## Praise for Jim McLean and the Eight-Step S...

"If I had to pick one teacher to take a lesson from, it would
— Ken Venturi, lead analyst f
U.S. Open Champion, 16 PGA T
Tom Watson, Tom Weiskopf, and John Cook

"Jim and his world-class staff are the best in the business. I love to visit all of his schools. You would love it, too. Read this book, and it may convince you to take the next step, going to a school."

—Len Mattiace, two-time PGA Tour Winner

"Jim McLean's work is the very best of its kind in the world of golf. He has developed models for understanding the golf swing that are based on his keen eye and attentive ear to the legendary players' swing habits and he has conjoined that with motor control research of the world's top contemporary players. No one has conducted such a thorough investigation of the golf swing from as many different perspectives with as many different research resources as Jim. The most experienced PGA Tour players will benefit as much as the average club player from this book."

—Dr. Fran Pirozzolo

"Jim McLean sees the golf swing as it is, not as he would like it to be. From playing at the highest level, to rigorous film study of every significant player of the last 75 years, to passionately seeking out golf's deepest thinkers, Jim brings an unparalleled wisdom to his analysis of every facet of the greatest game."

—Jaime Diaz, world-famous golf writer

"Having the privilege of watching him grow in this game has been a pleasure and he is the best at what he does."

—Jackie Burke, Masters Champion, PGA Champion,
five-time Ryder Cup Member, two-time Ryder Cup
Captain, PGA Hall of Fame

"I reached the #1 ranking in America for Junior boys. I started my golf lessons at the McLean school at Doral and still work with Jim and his staff. They are the best. Every time I stop at Doral I see great players, celebrities, or just a ton of amateurs all getting better at golf. It is the most fun golf range in the world."

—Erik Compton, ESPY Award Winner for Courage

# THE EIGHT-STEP
# SWING

**ALSO BY JIM McLEAN**

*The 3 Scoring Clubs*

*The Complete Idiot's Guide to Improving Your Short Game*

*Golf Digest's Book of Drills*

*Golf Digest's Ultimate Drill Book*

*The Golf School*

*The Wedge-Game Pocket Companion*

*The Power Game Pocket Companion*

*The Putter's Pocket Companion*

*The X-Factor Swing*

**The Top-Selling Swing System**

**That Has Revolutionized**

**the Teaching Industry**

## THIRD EDITION

# THE EIGHT-STEP
# SWING

FOREWORDS BY CRISTIE KERR AND TOM KITE

## JIM McLEAN

ILLUSTRATIONS BY PHIL FRANKE AND DOM LUPO
PHOTOGRAPHS BY JEFF BLANTON

**COLLINS**

*An Imprint of HarperCollins Publishers*

HarperCollins books may be purchased for educational, business, or sales promotional use. For information, please write: Special Markets Department, HarperCollins Publishers, 10 East 53rd Street, New York, NY 10022.

THIRD EDITION

*Designed by Ellen Cipriano*

Illustrations copyright © 1994 by Dom Lupo and © 2008 by Phil Franke

Photographs copyright © 1994 by Jeff Blanton and © 2000 by Henebry

The Library of Congress has catalogued the previous edition as follows:

McLean, Jim.
    The eight-step swing: the top-selling swing system that has revolutionized the teaching industry / Jim McLean.–2nd ed.
      p.  cm.
   ISBN 0-06-095800-6
   1. Swing (Golf)   I. Title: 8-step swing.   II. Title.
   GV979.S9 M32 2000
   796.352'3—dc21                                  00-058187

ISBN 978-0-06-167282-8

09  10  11  12  13  WBG/QWF  10  9  8  7  6  5  4  3  2  1

*This book is dedicated to my family:*

*Justine, Matt, and Jon. My wife, Justine, has supported my efforts and*

*stood by me as I traveled, studied, and moved forward in my career as*

*a golf instructor. My boys, Matt and Jon, are the light of my life—by*

*far the greatest thing ever to happen to me. I love you all.*

# CONTENTS

# FOREWORD TO THE THIRD EDITION

I've worked with Jim McLean since I was a little girl in Miami, Florida. I received a letter from Jim McLean welcoming me to the golf school at Doral and offering help if I ever needed it.

Jim opened up his arms and his golf school to me, and without that I would not have been able to become one of the best female golfers in the world. Jim helped me to become a student of the game and to want to learn about my own game, as well as studying the games of great players such as Sam Snead, Jackie Burke, Jack Nicklaus, Tiger Woods, Arnold Palmer, Ken Venturi, Annika Sorenstam, Juli Inkster, and many more. One of Jim's favorite sayings is "If you don't do the research, then you have nothing to teach."

That's what I always remember about Jim: his attention to detail and the ease with which he goes about teaching others. His wealth of knowledge is astounding. When others don't pick up on something, he finds it right away. I remember being at the golf school at Doral and sitting in on the staff meetings—yes, I was an assistant, too! Jim made us learn about different topics constantly, and he always challenged us to broaden our knowledge so we could apply it to teaching others or to our own golf game. His beliefs and the way in which he teaches the Eight-Step Swing produces the best instructors in the country consistently year after year.

Getting to spend time around Jim and watching him teach, I noticed one very amazing thing: He doesn't want to change you! He just tries to simplify what you have, to take you to the very best you can be—and by still being you. And he instills this in how he teaches his instructors.

I was fortunate to be able to meet many great professional golfers and sit in on a few lessons when Jim was teaching. I've been a student of Jim's philosophies and of the Eight-Step Swing since I was fifteen years old, and they have never let me down. I know that when you read this book you will find your own discoveries about golf and specifically your own golf swing. Use this proven system for your golf swing, and you will see amazing results.

There is no better way to learn about the golf swing than to read Jim McLean's new work and see for yourself how he totally differentiates himself and his school from all the others.

—*Cristie Kerr*
U.S. Open champion
Ten-time tour winner
Number One–ranked junior
Number One–ranked amateur
Number One–ranked professional in America
U.S. Curtis Cup team
Three-time Solheim Cup member

# FOREWORD TO THE SECOND EDITION

I cannot think of a more qualified person to be writing a book on advanced, quality golf instruction than Jim McLean. In my opinion, Jim has earned the right to author this book. Why? Plain and simple, he has the knowledge. Jim has gone the extra mile to talk to the top players and teachers and pick their brains for any tidbit of information that may help him become first, a better player and then, a better teacher. Jackie Burke, Gary Player, Harvey Penick, Paul Runyan, Ben Hogan, Bob Charles, Ben Crenshaw, Don January, Byron Nelson, Ken Venturi, Claude Harmon, and even I are only a few of those who have been quizzed by Jim.

But how one handles that knowledge has to be just as important. Jim has seen that there is not only one way to play the game. An experienced teacher knows that he or she must take what the student has and work within those limitations. He has fundamentals that support his teaching—fundamentals that are well supported by those players listed above. But he is not a "do it my way or else" kind of guy.

Jim has proved that with knowledge and versatility he can help students with a wide range of handicaps—everyone from the rank beginner to the veteran PGA Tour professional. This book will prove he also can help teachers improve their methods.

—*Tom Kite*
PGA Hall of Fame
U.S. Open champion
All-time leading money winner for a ten-year span
Ryder Cup captain
Played on seven Ryder Cup teams
U.S. Walker Cup member

# INTRODUCTION

*There's Madness to a Method*

*"The best way to show that a stick is crooked is not to argue about it or spend time denouncing it, but to lay a straight stick alongside it."*

—D.L. MOODY

This book is designed to be golf's straight stick. Let's finally separate fact from fiction. If you have been dissatisfied with your present instruction, read this book and learn exactly why.

You may have read about many miracle golf instruction methods over the years, perhaps very recently. My research shows that they are crooked sticks. No method works for all golfers, and some of the methods are only fit for a narrow sliver of the golf population. Yet they are marketed and sold to you as "one size fits all."

Fads and quick miracles pop up in every field, and few prove to last. In our culture, "here today, gone tomorrow" wisdom has become so common-place that no one seems offended if a fad doesn't actually work. New diet plans implore us to take this pill or replace this food with a new and specially developed substitute. But diets come and go as quickly as the seasons. The ones that last are the ones based on fundamental principles that include healthy foods, portion control, and exercise.

Method golf instruction is very similar to fad diets. Each season there is a new method or two that is guaranteed to produce the results you have been looking for. Set up like this, make sure the club does that on the backswing, change your backswing plane, put your left arm at an exact angle at the top, or use a brand-new release action. In golf, methods come on strong with marketing and promotion claims of having reinvented the golfing wheel. But after a short time they are almost always disproved and fade away. It doesn't mean that the next idea won't have a huge audience. Golfers are notorious for wanting an immediate cure, and they will often try just about anything. As a result, many golfers pay a lot of money only to get worse at ball striking and more frustrated with the game.

Methods in golf instruction, like diets, become popular because people are drawn to solutions that provide hope without a lot of mental or physical effort. Human beings want answers, but they would rather avoid the attention to detail and time that any truly effective process, done correctly, requires. We just want to follow a few easy directions and get fast results. We want to lose that thirty pounds in thirty days or gain that extra twenty yards off the tee in just a few days. Past experience and logic get put on hold in favor of the human compulsion for the quick fix. Jackie Burke said, "People think of losing pounds when they should be first starting to lose ounces."

The bad news for golfers is that swing methods are generally more counterproductive than diets. Rarely do diets cause people to actually gain weight. Most people will stay the same, improve slightly, or in some cases actually experience the dramatic weight loss that was advertised (at least temporarily). Golf swings are different. Three things can happen to a golf swing undergoing a change: status quo, improvement, or decline. The last result is the one the magazines don't talk about: the method that causes a five handicap to slip to a ten handicap or worse, the method that causes the elite player to fall from elite status. The PGA Tour player who tries a new swing method, loses his old swing, and is gone from the tour, never to regain his old form. Most of us have friends who have gone to a method teacher and never played as well again.

Almost always, golf methods fail. They fail for various reasons, the most basic being that they are founded on faulty information, and they don't make room for the idiosyncrasies and acceptable natural moves of individual human beings. The method's premise may well sound logical, and method teachers are great at giving absolute answers based on narrow criteria. But invariably the premise wasn't researched well enough, and the method teacher conveniently avoids seeing all the great players who are not doing what they teach.

True research begins with detailed observation. A scientist observes something within nature and wonders if this observation is true. The scientist then writes down a hypothesis and goes to the lab to test it. When in the lab, the scientist looks to control as many variables as possible. A controlled environment will help the scientist ultimately produce the most consistent results, which will either disprove or validate the hypothesis. With most so-called golf research, the basic scientific method described is not used. A method teacher will usually observe a particular move or concept that he interprets as key to the swing. Generally, pictures or opinions and testimonials from top players will be used to validate his point. All of these are nearly worthless for golf research. If they do use video, it is often shot from random locations and is therefore also not accurate or acceptable research. With that "evidence," the method teacher will proclaim that his swing is technically correct and based on sound research. My favorite excuse from a method teacher when presented with solid research that goes against his or her method is this: "My method is based on the Iron Byron swing machine. It's a perfect swing." While that's true, Iron Byron has one leg and one arm, hits off a perfectly flat surface, and has zero lateral motion.

The research I have seen for most methods is not professionally documented in any way—rendering it basically worthless. The pictures they show, when there are pictures, are from different angles and at different points in the swing. The by-product of poorly researched and failing methods is that many golfers get worse. The patient gets sicker.

That's why I have written this new book in conjunction with my Eight-Step Swing System. It is in hopes that I can shine a light on the madness by laying a straight stick right next to these methods. The straightness is attained through exhaustive research—getting video done precisely and correctly in a detailed fashion, and minutely studying hundreds of the top professional golfers worldwide. I believe I have used video differently and more correctly than any teacher. I believe golf is an art more than a science, but there is definitely science and geometry in a functionally sound golf swing. Art, like science, is best found in the details. After reading my material and my research, you can then logically decide what is truly important in your golf swing.

To clarify our video research, the camera must be placed in the correct location. It must be at the correct distance and height. Finally, we need to know where each particular shot went. To give you an idea of how difficult this is, I will tell you that it usually takes a young well-trained, college-educated teacher a minimum of three or four months to get decent at filming. It's not easy.

When our staff films at tour events, it is not uncommon for one of them to film for ten hours, getting dozens of different tour players. Yet, at the end of the day, only two or three clips might be useful. All the others might be slightly off. If we don't have the players perfectly in frame and with the perfect angles, the clip is thrown out. It cannot be used in our studies. If each swing were filmed differently, each swing would look slightly different, causing our research to be flawed at best. That's why we all film in precisely the same way. It is important for you to know that I have fifty-plus staff filming at many professional events in America and also overseas. It is also important to note that all my video clips are reviewed by my entire staff, not just me. I try to take all the bias out of the observations.

Total credit for how to properly research a golf swing and the unique way we analyze goes to my friend and fellow professional Carl Welty, a top fifty–

ranked teacher since the initial published rankings. Carl and I began working together back in the 1960s, well before I first started teaching at Westchester Country Club in New York. Of course, no one had video back then, so Carl was using 8-millimeter film. When I began professional instruction, I was teaching with something called a sequence camera. It printed out eight sequence pictures of the golf swing in under one minute. When Sony came out with the Betamax in 1978, Carl had perhaps the first one. Carl and I set out to find commonalities among the game's greatest players, and our lab was outdoors in the real world of the best players. Instead of using pictures and quotes and opinions, we used video to prove and disprove our many hypotheses on the golf swing. In order to control the number of variables, we filmed each swing the same way every time. Doing this, we also noted what the ball did on each swing. This exhaustive database was the foundation of our research. We often watched video until 2:00 or 3:00 a.m. night after night, and together we began to see just how wrong many swing theories and swing concepts were. We learned that much of what we ourselves believed and were teaching to students was simply not required to hit great golf shots, and the top players were not doing what many teachers said they did.

The ideas for this book provide accurate "answers" based on top-notch research. Our database is huge, with all the golf swings of past and current top tour players, and it is not slanted. What it proves is that a golf swing does not have to attain so-called perfect positions in order to be correct. Rather, there is a range for these positions that allows them to be correct, depending on what works and repeats for an individual player. Because no two people are exactly alike—physically, emotionally, or temperamentally—no two swings are the same. Teaching one method to every student obviously should not work, and of course it does not. The greatest golf swings in history all have differences that—based on their results—are acceptable.

In addition, since I last updated *The Eight-Step Swing* in 2001, our research has continued to develop. I hired Dr. Rob Neal, who worked in Australia for twenty-two years in biomechanics and with the Australian Institute of Sport, that country's top golf training program. Rob came to Doral in 2003, and together we have researched the swings of hundreds of regular amateur students attending my golf schools. With biomechanics we have learned even more about improving golf swings. In addition, Rob has had U.S. Open champions and many other tour players on the bio machine we use both at Doral and in Texas. I keep working with Rob to improve our corridors and safety zones for every part of the body motions.

What our research continues to show is that there are actually very few "perfect" golf swing positions. There is really only one area where top players look most alike, and that is from transition to shoulder height on the forward swing, or from what I term Step Five through Step Seven. It's certainly not the backswing that makes a great golf swing, since every backswing on every tour is different. If you don't believe me, I hope you will simply take the time to check it out yourself. As Claude Harmon, one of the top teachers I have known and worked with extensively, has said, "It's not how you back the car out of the garage." Claude knew that many varying backswings could produce great golf shots if you got the forward part correct. When things got too scientific, Claude would say, "Whatever happened to a square face at impact?" Never has a truer sentence ever been uttered!

One of the greatest ball strikers who ever lived—Johnny Miller—shares this view. He once told me during a clinic we did together many years ago in Mexico that the golf swing is overrated. By Miller's definition, if a player can hit great shots consistently under pressure, then he or she has a great golf swing. That explains how Lee Trevino, Jim Furyk, and Lorena Ochoa, three players with three swings as dramatically different from each other as you could imagine, could all hit consistently wonderful golf shots when it counts and win majors. I laugh when I hear TV commentators say all of the modern players have homogenized swings: "They are all the same." That is very lazy reporting. I don't know what they are looking at. I say the exact opposite: they are all different!

The truth is, **perfect for you will always be unique to you.** The best road for achieving adequate speed, correct path, and solid contact comes by improving body positions, body angles, and body motions, and syncing the arms and hands to create solid contact, maximum power, and accuracy. There's no argument that understanding correct positions and movements of your body will allow you to have much more control, more power, and the ability to repeat. These are keys to great ball striking.

But the way you get there, and the way it will look after you do, will be individual. You may use a non-release or a release action (arms and hands). Most golfers will use a combination of the two. This book will give you real answers. You will learn ranges and how to stay within safety zones, and it's within those areas that you can find real and lasting improvement. To own your golf swing is to keep your own good qualities while incorporating better technique where you need it. This book will show you not a method, but your own way to golf success.

# THE EIGHT-STEP
# SWING

# THE FUNDAMENTALS AND ANTI-FUNDAMENTALS OF GOLF

*Jim McLean's Twenty-two Fundamentals for Great
Ball Striking, and Twenty-five Misconceptions of the Golf Swing*

As a teacher of the game for more than thirty years, I've made hundreds of friends in my profession. I've learned from many, and I've trained many. But I must report that there is still a tremendous amount of misinformation being propagated by golf instructors. Frankly, I seriously thought, when I first published the true fundamentals of top ball striking in *The Eight-Step Swing* more than a decade ago, that it would be a huge deal in the teaching world. To my surprise, almost no one noticed. That's why this time I lead with them in Chapter 1.

Often the information you read or watch on TV is just dead wrong. Sometimes the information is partially correct for a certain segment of golfers but will mislead and damage many others who try to employ this new way of swinging. "Partially correct" is a good definition for most swing methods. It's the part that is "partially incorrect" that can do serious damage. In golf instruction, a little off is way off.

Mainly, teachers around the world continue to teach their opinions. As a result, they continue to spread as truth positions and movements that many great players simply do not do.

If any writer or golf publication would seriously look at the number of players who reached a very high amateur ranking or who made it to the PGA Tour but were then ruined or damaged their game for many years by using a strict method (perhaps taught by well-known teachers), it would shock the golf world. Even tour players are subject to trying a miracle method. Just like you, a good number of supertalented golfers will try some new method that has "all the answers." It's an amazing thing! Quite a few gifted golfers have ended up on the junk heap of golf oblivion by changing their natural swing. They were likely taking things out of their golf swing that did not need changing, and as a result they got worse. Later they might find out that several of the greatest ball strikers in history were doing exactly the same thing that they took out. You just cannot teach every person the same swing. There is no one perfect swing. As teachers, we have to adjust to the student, not the other way around. Sadly, this does not always happen.

At the same time, many teachers claim as their own discovery technically correct information that is as much as a century old. To put this into golf instruction, there is no new miracle swing but rather old ideas that are repackaged. Very little is really new, except to golfers who simply do not know golf history. As President Harry Truman once wrote, "The only thing new in the world is the history you don't know."

The sad thing for students is that these same instructors will often be teaching something entirely different next year—or in some cases, next month. They are in search mode just like many students. Many teachers go from one method to another and simply will not do any research on their own.

Any serious student of the game is looking for constants. What do the best players actually *do*? Those are the things that can be accurately called the fundamentals. But you would be surprised by how many things that have been long and respectfully considered fundamentals actually aren't. And that the real fundamentals are hardly even known. Remember—real fundamentals are what all top ball strikers have in common, not what some uninformed person claims is a perfect golf swing. I say: Prove it. Show me who does it. Don't tell me; show me.

Ask almost every teaching pro in the world to name four fundamentals, and they will repeat what they have been taught from their PGA associations. Usually it is grip, aim, posture, and stance. Well, I can guarantee you that these are absolutely not fundamentals to great ball striking or to becoming a great player.

Let me give you just a few easy examples. The man most knowledgeable golfers would consider having the greatest golf swing of all time, Sam Snead, slumped his shoulders and leaned out toward the ball (as does 2007 U.S. Open champion Angel Cabrera), which is far from the perfect posture. A straight line down from Snead's shoulders would hit in front of his toes. Sam also aimed to the right of his target and took the club away to the inside, "under" the shaft plane. In recent times, Zach Johnson won the 2007 Masters with one of the strongest grips you could ever find, carrying his hands as low as any top golfer in history, similar to Hubert Green and Fuzzy Zoeller (both multiple major champions). Zach also lifts up dramatically in the backswing and returns the clubshaft on a much higher plane at impact. Lee Trevino aimed a hundred yards to the left and pushed his shots far out to the right of where his body was aligned. He also had an extremely strong left-hand grip. Yet, most observers who saw them both would say that the quality of Trevino's ball striking was the equal of Ben Hogan's. Hogan, by the way, had a very weak grip, as did major champions Johnny Miller and Bill Rogers, as well as many modern-day PGA Tour players. Tiger Woods has dramatically weakened his left-hand grip in the past few years, showing just one knuckle. Many golfers look at Sergio Garcia, one of the greatest ball strikers of the past decade, and see another odd swing. Instead, I search to see all the things he is doing right.

The so-called "correct" grip is probably the actual non-fundamental that is most commonly considered a fundamental. The truth is that all of us have different hand sizes, hand features, and grip strengths. You practice to find a grip that works for you—meaning one that gets the clubface square at impact with speed and with excellent impact alignments. As I will repeat over and over in this book, the critical part of any golf swing is **the impact zone—from waist high to waist high (Step Five through Step Seven).** If you are great in this area and you can repeat it, then your golf swing is great. Period.

Regarding the grip, consider the adjoining box that lists a few of the great players who use so-called unusual grips.

### REVERSE DOUBLE OVERLAP GRIP

Jim Furyk (U.S. Open champion)

Steve Jones (1996 U.S. Open champion)

### DOUBLE OVERLAP VARDON

Camilo Villegas (tour championship winner 2008)

### MESH GRIP, NO OVERLAP

Greg Norman (Hall of Fame)

### TEN FINGER

Jane Geddes (U.S. Open champion)

Beth Daniel (Hall of Fame)

Bob Estes (tour winner, ranked Number One in Greens in Regulation for a full year on the PGA Tour)

Dave Barr (tour winner)

Bob Rosburg (PGA champion)

## INTERLOCKING

Tiger Woods (four-time Masters champion, three-time U.S. Open champion,
  four-time PGA champion, ranked Number One in the world)

Jack Nicklaus (Hall of Fame; 18 majors)

Nancy Lopez (Hall of Fame)

Tom Kite (U.S. Open champion, Hall of Fame)

Bruce Lietzke (14-time tour winner, Ryder Cup player, U.S. Senior Open champion)

## SUPER STRONG

Judy Rankin (Hall of Fame)

Paul Azinger (ranked Number Two in the world)

Fred Couples (Masters champion)

Ed Fiori (six-time tour winner)

David Duval (ranked Number One in the world)

## SUPER WEAK

José Maria Olazabal (two major championships)

Bill Rogers (ranked Number One in the world)

Joe Durant (multiple winner on tour, Number One GIR)

Heck, three players have won the Masters with their left thumb "off the club." I'm not saying I don't think the grip is important, or that at our schools we don't normally teach most students a fairly "standard" grip. We check each student, and we look for irregularities that might be the cause of poor shots, but we adjust for a person's idiosyncrasies. The key point here is that there is no correct perfect grip for everyone. A certain grip, even endorsed by the PGA of America or anyone else, simply is not a fundamental.

The surprising truth is that not one in a hundred golf instructors can list true golf fundamentals for top-class ball striking. I know because I've heard the answers from professionals in my audiences. So many of them don't know, but they are still out on the lesson tee day after day, teaching something and passing information that may not benefit their students and often just repeating clichés.

Other examples of things uninformed teachers consider fundamental "constants" include the "turn," "square clubface at the top," aim, "balance," "pull the club down from the top," "turn in a barrel," or ideas along these lines. While I obviously agree that sometimes these ideas are excellent tips, **they are simply and absolutely not top ball striking fundamentals**.

Through my association with Carl Welty and many years of additional research with a top-notch teaching staff, we are solid on what the true fundamentals are, and I know what they aren't. The following are twenty-five misconceptions and non-fundamentals that many teachers—and, by extension, golfers—continue to hold on to at their peril. Incorporating any of these ideas into your swing can possibly ruin your chances of hitting good shots consistently.

1. "Your head is a stationary post." (*No.* Your head moves. All top players have head movement. No one freezes the head.)
2. "Stay in your spine angle from start to finish." (*No.* All good players stand up somewhat going into the finish position.)
3. "Your left heel must not rise off the ground in the backswing." (*No.* Many PGA Tour players lift the heel in the backswing. Also included in the raise-the-heel camp are Nicklaus, Snead, Hogan, Jones, Irwin, Miller, Mickelson, and Watson. In fact, nearly 40 percent of the PGA Tour lift the left heel in the backswing with a driver, and beyond that a surprisingly high number have the heel off the ground at impact.)
4. "Swing in a barrel." (*No.* Your hips do not turn in a perfect circle.)

The old idea of swinging in a barrel just does not fly. No great ball striker turns in a perfect circle or inside a barrel. We use the idea of swinging in a barrel only for golfers with too much lateral sway.

LATERAL MOTION

Bust the barrel for the correct sequence and a true power move.

5. "Set up parallel to the target line." (*No.* Lots of great players set up off the line, both left and right. More set up left.)

6. "Keep your feet in place" or "your back foot should not slide." (*No.* Tell that to Davis Love, Nicklaus, Couples, Hogan, Littler, Norman, Casper, and Cabrera, to name just a few. In fact, you would probably be better off learning to slide the back foot, rather than just going up onto the right toe and keeping the back foot in place.)

7. "Set your wrists at a ninety-degree angle when the left arm is parallel to the ground." (*Beyond ridiculous.* It leaves out Snead, Nicklaus, Woods, Norman, and many others.)

8. "Keep your left arm straight." (*No.* Less than 5 percent of the entire PGA Tour keeps the left arm straight in a driver swing.)

9. "Fold your right elbow against your right side in the take-away." (*A very old wives' tale.* Nobody does this.)

10. "Start with your hands ahead of the ball for all shots." (*No.* On the contrary, hand position and shaft angle vary from shot to shot. Most great drivers actually have the hands behind the ball at setup.)

11. "Address and impact are similar." (*No.* They're not even close.)

12. "Grip position must be a certain way." (*No.* The grip is only a connection of the golfer to the club. A great grip returns the clubface to square at impact. That means it can be different from player to player.)

13. "Golf is a left-sided game." (*No.* On the contrary, many great ball strikers are very right-side-dominant: Venturi, Peete, Sutton, Hogan, Leonard. The best players use their dominant side, and some even focus on the dominant side. Golf is a two-sided game. It's okay to focus on either side, or both sides.)

14. "The hands and arms supply most of the power." (*No.* Try this: Sit with your feet off the ground, no shoulder turn allowed, and tell me how far you hit it. With your feet off the ground you lose the second critical connection in golf, which is your feet to the ground.)

15. "There is a perfect position at the top." (*No.* As Jackie Burke once asked me, "How stupid are you?" Take the top five money winners each year for the past century, and every year you'll see five different positions at the top.)

16. "Take the club straight off the ball and swing down the line." (*No.* What really should happen is that the club swings in a circle around the body. Therefore, you attack the ball from the inside to hit it straight. After impact, the clubhead arcs back to the inside of the target line and does not swing straight at the intended target.)

17. "Keep your head down after impact." (*No.* Do this and you guarantee slow swing speeds and an inevitable back injury. You're practicing being a nonathlete when you keep your head down.)

18. "There is one ball position for all clubs." (*No.* Golf is, of course, played outdoors. All great ball strikers adjust ball position for shots hit into a strong wind, downwind, specialty shots, and various curve shots.)

19. "Release the club immediately from the top." (This advice is okay as long as at one and the same time you make a powerful shift to the front leg. Unfortunately, most golfers cannot do this. The result is fat or skulled shots. When you hit the ball solid, it is high and weak. Most high-handicappers cast from the top, exactly what we do not want to have happen.)

20. "Release equals hand action." (*No.* Actually, *release* refers to your entire right side releasing toward the target. The right hand covers the left well after impact. Thinking of release as just hand action is just beginner golf talk.)

21. "The right heel must be on the ground at impact." (*No.* On the contrary, Woods, Singh, Els, Nicklaus, and just about all other top players have air under the right heel at impact for full shots. On the PGA Tour, 95 percent of players have the right heel off the ground at impact with a full swing.)

22. "The clubface must be toe up halfway back." (*No.* There are hundreds of exceptions by the best players.)

23. "You must swing inside out." (*No.* This is a concept that can greatly help average golfers, but top ball strikers do not swing inside out. It's an absolute killer for a tournament player. If you see your divots going out to the right of the target, save your money and don't enter any tournaments.)

24. "You must be looking at the ball when you hit it." (*No.* Think about Durant, Sorenstam, Stenson, Warren, and Furyk.)

25. "If you swing left, the ball will start left. If you swing right, the ball will start on that line to the right." (*No.* The fact is that the ball will never go where you swing unless the clubface is at a ninety-degree angle to the path. The nine possible ball flights taught by the American PGA are hopelessly incorrect.)

Whew! It's amazing to consider the sheer volume of all the incorrect things golfers have taken as gospel, isn't it?

Okay, so let's apply our straight stick. Here, for the second time, are the real fundamentals of top-class ball striking. Although I have updated the list and added several fundamentals with our continuing and ongoing research, these McLean Fundamentals are all based on the tremendous amount of research I've already mentioned. They are the swing motions we've found that all great ball strikers have in common. They are what we check for in every golfer who comes to our golf schools. There are twenty-two of them, and I can assure you that all of them hold up to the most rigorous examination. Consider them, think about them, challenge them. I hope they stick in golf's memory.

1. **Center contact.** Top players consistently hit the sweet spot. I never go to the lesson tee without my impact tape. When was the last time you checked your impact? Do you have any idea how crucial it is to

hit the center of the clubface? Contact will control spin, launch angle, distance, curve, and your perception of what happened in your golf swing.

2. **There are four main power sources: hands (wrists), arms, weight shift, and rotation.** There are, of course, many other parts of the body and twelve joints that we could list as power producers, but when I show my students the four power sources, they get it easier.

3. **A two-pivot-point swing.** Both legs hit the ground, and we use both of them. For power swings, we coil into the back leg and hit off the front leg. This shifting action creates a slight U-shaped flat spot at the bottom of the swing arc. Weight shift also allows the clubhead to stay closer to the target line for a longer period of time. A one–pivot point swing uses the head as the swing center and a coil around a fixed spine location (unlike the legs, the spine does not reach the ground). Players with a longer flat spot at the bottom of the swing arc tend to be the better ball strikers—and the flat spot in a one–pivot point swing is shorter than in a two–pivot point swing. You can play either way. Jones, Nelson, Hogan, Snead, Player, Nicklaus, Seve, Faldo, Watson, Trevino, Price, and Woods used the two pivot points and lateral shift. All would reach the Number One ranking in the world.

4. **There is lateral motion.** The hips shift just slightly away from the target on the backswing (for 95 percent of all tour players). Going forward, there is a more visible lateral shift. On a full golf swing of a right-handed golfer swinging the longer clubs, the bottom of the spine moves toward the right as the right leg becomes the backswing pivot point, or post. A power hitter, in particular, lines up—or stacks—the majority of his weight on his right side during the backswing. A note here: On a short iron or wedge shot, or for low flight shots, the top ball striker might stay centered, with no shifting.

Without any question, you can play this way, but it is not a power move or a natural athletic move. Some teachers would disagree with my research on backswing movement (even though players like Ben Hogan wrote about that slight lateral backswing motion). Very few, but not all, teachers would disagree with a significant lateral move in the forward swing. Any teacher that cannot see this simply has done no study of top players. I will describe in detail this transition move and the lateral move in Step Five.

5. **The head moves in the golf swing.** It goes where the body takes it. The head either rotates or shifts laterally or does a combination of both in the backswing. Interestingly, even the greatest players will say or write that they do not move the head. One of my all-time golf heroes, Jack Nicklaus, is one of them. Yet, when you study Jack on video, his head moves. Jack moves his chin three or four inches away from the target and rotates his head almost forty-five degrees. Also, a straight line drawn directly through the top of his head clearly shows lateral motion when Jack was hitting his driver, and when he was clearly the Number One player in the world. Watch what the greats do, not necessarily what they say. It is important to note that Jack is left-eye dominant. Left-eye dominant golfers can turn the head away from the target and still see the ball. Right-eye dominant golfers will not rotate the head nearly as much, but they may have more lateral motion.

6. **When the hands get to waist height on the backswing, the right arm is even or above the left.** This is with the camera set at chest height.

7. **The shoulders out-turn the hips in the backswing.**

8. **The hips do not stay on a level rotation in the backswing or forward swing.** The right hip goes slightly up on the backswing, and the hipline rises through impact and to the finish. The hips do not turn level, as is advocated by numerous books and methods. The hipline

is higher at impact and at the finish than when the golfer starts the downswing. During the impact segment, the left hip will be considerably higher than the right hip. The hipline is at its lowest as the golfer starts down in a sit-down position, but rises from there to past impact in a huge power move. I learned a great deal about the power created by this hip rise through my many lessons and talks with Jimmy Ballard, who was very innovative with this part of the golf swing—and was often misunderstood.

9. **The hips change axis.** The hips also change axis during the swing. This means that the front hip (the left hip for the right-hander) rises even more in the impact zone. It is only at the finish of the swing that the hips become level.

10. **In all great ball strikers, the downswing arc is narrower than the backswing arc.** Many a method will focus on a perfect swing plane, and will teach that the backswing and the downswing match up the swing arc. The idea is to put the club on the ideal arc going back and then match that exact arc on the downswing. No great ball striker does this. Always remember that you want the downswing arc well inside the backswing arc. Every great ball striker does this. There is a plane shift in all great swings: two planes, one going back and one coming down. They are not the same!

11. **In transition, starting the downswing, the right elbow leads the right hand.** As we check the crucial transition move of all top ball strikers, we see that each has the right elbow leading the action. A key move.

12. **Clubhead speed.** All great ball strikers have excellent swing speed. Here is a true fundamental to top ball striking that is often not recognized. Without sufficient speed, nobody can be a top-level professional ball striker. Speed changes the game of golf.

13. **With a driver swing, the head is well behind the ball at impact.** Interestingly, and unknown to most teachers, is the fact that the head

moves differently (for most top ball strikers) with a driver. In iron shots, most top ball strikers will have the head return near the original position or slightly forward of that position. With the driver, you see the head move behind where it was at address, because of both ball position and the ball being teed. Most great ball strikers also compress the body and head lower than the address position.

14. **The upper part of the forward arm (left arm for the right-handed golfer) is connected to the body during and past impact.** A very common error in average golfers occurs when the left arm separates from the body in a cutting action, or chicken-wing move—a major power leak.

15. **The shoulders, upper center, arms, and club rotate in unison past impact.** This was one of the very first fundamentals Carl Welty showed me on film. It was startling to see the difference between the greats and the not-so-greats. Poor or inconsistent ball strikers are out of sync, often with hip or shoulder rotation stalling out through impact.

16. **The left (or forward) wrist is flat or slightly bowed at impact.** This means that for iron shots, the bottom of your golf swing must be well ahead of the ball by several inches. For a teed-up driver, the shaft will return more in a straight line, and not leaning as much forward as the iron shot. Many great drivers like Nicklaus, Norman, Montgomerie, Lietzke, Garcia, Cabrera, and Sorenstam have no forward lean at all. Remember—there is a significant difference in driving and full shots with longer clubs compared to short iron swings. To clarify the flat left wrist, it is possible to hit great shots by returning the wrist to the setup angle, but you must never increase the cup of the left wrist from your address position for power golf shots.

17. **The right heel (the back heel) leads the toe of the right foot at the start of the downswing.** Not all top ball strikers have the right heel off the ground at impact on a full swing, but a huge majority do. More than

95 percent of all tour players have air under their right foot at impact with a full power swing (not a short iron shot). This is the only McLean Fundamental that is not closer to 100 percent, for every top tour play.

18. **The lead arm and the lead knee (left arm and left knee) are forward of their address position at impact.** Many high-handicap golfers and weak ball strikers do not achieve this more forward position.

19. **The upper center of the body is more forward at impact on all iron shots than it was at address.** Upper center—not just the lower center—moves forward from the address position in great ball strikers hitting irons. A high percentage of tour players have upper center forward of address position with all clubs. A smaller percentage of top ball strikers have their upper center slightly back when using drivers and when the ball is teed.

20. **At impact the hips are more open to the target than the shoulders.** Since the shoulders far out-turn the hips in the backswing, plus the hips start the downswing, there is a huge differential between the hips and the shoulders during transition, with the hips far ahead. That gap will close dramatically once the player has made the initial shift and turn of the hips—but the hips will still be slightly ahead of the shoulders at impact. Many amateurs do just the opposite, with the shoulders leading the hips.

21. **Everything at address (setup) is different at impact.** The old idea was to turn and return to the same position or to set up by simulating impact. Both of these are fallacies. A dynamic impact position achieves proper impact angles and power body positions.

22. **There is some tilt of the upper body toward the ball's target line at the finish.** Top players do not finish straight up and down. A line drawn up from the center of the belt through the center of the head (looking down the target line) will always angle slightly toward the target line.

I believe these twenty-two fundamentals are a vital contribution to the game of golf. These are the fundamentals my instructors look at as we teach our students how to improve their ball striking. What is so important about them is that they give any serious teacher (and student) a true baseline to measure both correct technique and real progress. It has taken Carl Welty and me over thirty years to complete this information, plus huge help from the great teachers who have worked for me over many years.

It is so critical to know both lists and to focus your attention on the points relating specifically to your game. You might be very surprised to learn things you need not concern yourself with, along with one or two definite keys for improvement of your ball striking. Focus your attention on the swing elements that truly make a difference in ball striking.

# 2

# THE JIM McLEAN SYSTEM

*An Overview of the Entire McLean Program, Including the 25 Percent Theory*

I've always been involved in sports and highly interested in how the best

coaches got the most out of their players. I've made it a major goal in my

career to spend time and learn from some of the greatest coaches in and out

of golf. Outside the game, I've had the privilege of having contact with greats

like John Wooden, Angelo Dundee, Pat Riley, Bobby Knight, Bruce Coslet,

and Bill Belichick.

All were repositories of wisdom. I spent several days watching Angelo working with Muhammad Ali before his title fight with Buster Mathis, and I was fascinated by the way the trainer would impart advice to Ali amid all the seeming chaos that seemed to pervade the champion's camp. Actually it was Angelo and Bundini Brown who both stuck close to Ali and pelted him with positive input by the second. Ali listened because he knew that Angelo understood his strengths and weaknesses better than anyone else, and Bundini was assisting Angelo with his encouragement.

I spent many hours with Coach Wooden, who won ten NCAA Championships at UCLA and is arguably the greatest coach who ever lived in any sport. He left me with many lessons, but one I remember in particular was his observation that the greatest performers are originals, and he treated his players differently, not the same. He was always aware that many opposing coaches tried to copy his system and could seem like virtual replicas of his Bruin teams. I have had the same concerns with my system and ideas being used by others, often with no credit given. But he said that coaches who infused their teams with their own ideas were actually more difficult to play against than those who copied him. He knew that nobody could exactly copy everything he taught.

I realized that this idea was the core of my advice to all young talented players: Be yourself. It's perfectly fine for a young golfer to watch great players and imitate some aspects of their game. I encourage this. However, one thing I have seen as a player and a teacher is that when someone tries to copy another golfer's swing exactly (and often from a golf instructor), it never works. The copy is never quite as good as the original, and that young golfer has stopped being himself. I believe great players are copied by other players; they don't exactly copy someone else. It's a law of nature. Think of it this way: If it could be done, everyone would hit it like Ben Hogan. Many have tried to copy Hogan or Nicklaus. It has never worked.

My influences inside the game are almost too numerous to mention, but there have definitely been some key figures. I've already mentioned Carl Welty, my close friend and collaborator over more than thirty-five years.

Jimmy Ballard was the first great golf school instructor and the one who really set the path for golf teachers to be considered top coaches as they are in other sports. Nobody was better organized than Jimmy, and many modern teachers have stolen his material with no credit. He is the most criticized yet most misunderstood teacher I have ever known. Literally hundreds of tour players paid to go through a school with Jimmy. That has never happened before, and I doubt it will ever happen again.

Then there are the amazing people who were both great players and great teachers. Ken Venturi, the 1964 U.S. Open champion, so generously passed on to me what he learned from his close associations with both Ben Hogan and Byron Nelson. Johnny Revolta, the winner of eighteen PGA Tour events, and Claude Harmon, the 1947 Masters champion, were both teachers I worked closely with, as well as former U.S. Women's amateur champion, LPGA winner, and Harvey Penick protégé Mary Lena Faulk. Gardner Dickinson worked under Ben Hogan as his assistant at Tamarisk Country Club. Later, I would become the Director of Golf at Tamarisk Country Club. They were lifelong friends. Gardner won nineteen times on the PGA Tour. I played and worked on my game with Gardner at Frenchman's Creek in Palm Beach Gardens in Florida. Bob Toski, who won five times on the PGA Tour, is one of the greatest instructors ever, and we had great discussions on the golf swing every time we played together. I taught at Westchester Country Club with Lighthorse Harry Cooper, a member of the PGA Hall of Fame. Last is my great friend Jackie Burke, Jr., five-time Ryder Cup player, a Ryder Cup captain, a Masters champion, a PGA champion, and a Hall of Famer. I watched all these men teach many different types of players, and I took hundreds of lessons from them myself and played golf with them as well.

I learned many things from these great players who also taught the game: a compendium of knowledge that I draw from every day. None of them taught a method; they all taught the individual. But perhaps the most important lesson I learned from all my mentors is that a teacher has to have a framework that allows him organize all the myriad ideas that he accumulates in his lifetime. In short, a great teacher needs a SYSTEM.

A system differs from a method in that it allows much more flexibility to teach individuals. All the players and teachers I mentioned above are able to create concepts or systems that allowed the individuals they were instructing, with all different abilities and talents, to improve and thrive. That's my goal as a teacher of golf: to have the knowledge and the experience to adjust my teaching so that it takes best advantage of every particular person's abilities and talents. That's what I expect from all the fine teachers working at my schools. We are all on the same page, all singing off the same sheet of music, knowing there is flexibility in the Jim McLean System.

It took me a long time to develop my own system for teaching the game, because early on I was experimenting with so many different things. I started teaching full time in 1975 at Westchester Country Club, and for five years I gave a tremendous amount of lessons. Each winter I traveled America to spend time with different top teachers in virtually every part of the country. I took lessons from every teacher with any kind of reputation. I sat down with them, talked to them, took notes, and videotaped the sessions or used an audiocassette. Many of those teachers became good friends I could call on any time for anything I might need in golf. I'm pretty sure no other teacher has taken as many lessons as I have.

The turning point for me was in 1982, when I was first asked to make a major presentation to fellow golf professionals. I was forced to articulate my ideas on the game of golf and how I taught them, and this directly led me to develop my 25 Percent Theory. A big moment in gaining command as a teacher came when I delivered that two-hour presentation of my teaching concepts at the Metropolitan PGA Education Forum in New York before about three hundred teachers.

The 25 Percent Theory was something that had come to me during my years of playing on professional tours. It was my way to define the game and the separate components I needed to play the PGA Tour, my primary goal as a player. Although I was able to play in a few U.S. Opens and played in the Masters once, most of my career was spent on minitours, national and sectional club pro events, the Canadian tour, and scattered tour events. I was never able to get on the PGA Tour full time, and that only intensified my examination of what was needed.

My thought process was that there were actually several key areas to look at *that determine your total game.* At first, I did not know how much weight to give each one, but I knew that there was more to golf than the long game and the short game. I added the mental game, and then I added the management game. Upon closer inspection, I gave all four areas equal weight.

This became the cornerstone and centerpiece to all my teaching at my golf schools. I know that for an advanced tournament player, the mental game is by far the most important element of the four. I know that for the beginner, hitting the golf ball is the most important aspect of golf. We all know that improving the short game lowers our scores on the golf course and that some people build a strategy around their personal strengths and weaknesses much better than others. Often, less gifted players can shoot low scores by being mentally tough, being mentally alert, and making no mistakes in managing the course and themselves. You need to understand that improvement can come from any of the four key areas. I suggest that you honestly assess your strengths and weaknesses by using the 25 percent idea.

## THE LONG GAME

This encompasses your ball striking and the full swing. The long game is the full shots and the golf swing itself, which this book will define in great detail. I believe there are excellent ideas on these subjects that may well benefit you. Going to the range, hitting golf balls, working on your golf swing, becoming a better ball striker, and hitting the ball in the center of the clubface more often—these are the areas where most golfers spend their time and where they want to take instruction. For most people, they make up the most fun parts of practicing golf, because there is nothing quite like the all-out joy of a long, solid hit. But it's easy to get too caught up in the long game and forget that it's still only one piece of the total game. The allure of great ball striking is so seductive that people erroneously believe if they can build a perfect golf swing, they'll play perfect golf. Even if a person could perfect the long game—which no one has ever done or will do—there are still three other areas of golf to master. The long game is critically important, but to be a complete player you must immerse yourself just as much in the other three parts of the game.

## MORE ON PUTTING

My view on putting is that it changes the game. A great putter is always a threat, while a bad putter will never be a scorer. A great putt at the right time can totally turn a round. Putting influences the mental game because a great putter always feels he has a chance.

A great putter takes pressure off every other part of your game. You can be more aggressive with your iron game, knowing that you don't need a perfect bunker shot or chip to save par. You can play more conservatively and to the middle of greens, having no fear of three putting. So it is not the actual percentage of putts (outside of three feet) per round, but rather the importance of holing putts for continuing to start or build momentum or to hold on to momentum.

Putting is the ground game of golf, while ball striking is played in the air. The ground game wears opponents out and usually keeps the play "in" any round of golf. Great putting is mostly an art form, a mental game, and a confidence game. While technique can be important, there are more different putting methods that work than we could ever list. There is no one way to great putting, but believing in your technique is crucial.

A perfect example of how we teach the game of golf translates into my view on putting technique. I have had the wonderful opportunity to know and play many times with Ben Crenshaw, whom most tour players regard as the best putter of all time. I worked a decade with Brad Faxon during a stretch when he was the best statistically in golf. At that same time, I taught Lenny Mattiace, who won the World Putting Championship and was, again, highly regarded as a top putter by his peers on the PGA Tour.

Here is something you can take to the bank: all tour players have different putting strokes and other things that make each unique. Can you imagine that even the smallest stroke in golf is different from player to player? Ben used a short flange putter his entire career, with a long flowing backstroke and a shorter follow-through. He took the putter to the inside and hit very high on the ball, imparting a slightly upward motion and obviously a perfect roll. Faxon used a longer putter and set up with his left shoulder extremely high. Faxon used an arc-type stroke and had a super-smooth action. He lined up his ball by drawing a straight line on the ball as an aiming guide. Mattiace used a simple teeter-totter shoulder stroke. Unlike Crenshaw or Faxon, Lenny had his eyes directly over the ball-target line. His stroke was straight back and straight through. He also was very even in length of stroke, meaning that his backswing and follow-through matched.

The most popular putting teachers today could not be more opposite or further apart in their methods. Dave Pelz teaches zero blade rotation. Stan Utley teaches a major arc stroke and a slightly downward strike. Stan will often have his students putt with a three iron. This obviously gets the ball much farther away from the toe line and greatly encourages an arc motion. Who is right? In my philosophy they are both right. It only depends on the student. At my golf schools we teach a wide variety of putting strokes because I know this is probably the "most unique" part of the game. My instructors are taught to watch the ball, much more than the exact putting stroke. If the golfer rolls the ball perfectly, if he or she can start the ball consistently on the line they choose, and they can repeat it, then I like that stroke for that student. From there we focus extremely hard on "reading greens," an aspect of putting that I find heavily underestimated.

This is not a putting book, but I wanted to at least touch on the philosophy I employ. In doing so, I believe it gives you a better understanding of how I teach the full swing. The key is to look at what is truly important. There is no one perfect method in putting except the method and style that works for you. My job is to show you how this is done.

## THE SHORT GAME

I define the short game area from seventy-five yards in for mid- to high-handicappers and from a hundred yards in for better players. This includes putting, chipping, pitching, bunker play, and getting up and down from trouble within range. Since the best players in the game don't hit even 75 percent of the greens in regulation, you can see how important the short game is. Unquestionably, this is the area where students at our golf schools lower their scores the fastest. That is in part because the small pitching stroke contains the fundamental elements of your full swing. The pitch shot is truly a lost art. It is a shot we teach endlessly at all of my golf schools. If it is possible for you, the golf course is the best place to practice your short game. Most people certainly do not spend enough time on the short game.

## THE MANAGEMENT GAME

This is simply having the knowledge and discipline to manage yourself (your golf and your life). That means preparing yourself in every way possible in order to reach your goals. This might include a fitness program, better diet, and perhaps taking a more leisurely route getting to the golf course. It also means managing your game around the course, to avoid trouble and take the safe route, to avoid an unwise gamble. On the other hand, evaluating the circumstances of your match or the tournament may force you to take high risks, to focus on hitting the green rather than firing at dangerous hole locations, and to use a pre-shot routine effectively. In other words, the management game enables you to play golf intelligently rather than foolishly.

Improvement in these last two areas might reduce scores more than any improvement you can make in the physical areas. When we look at who was the greatest manager of the game and their life in the history of the game, it would probably be Jack Nicklaus and now Tiger Woods. Jack would analyze the golf course better than anyone. He had a complete game plan. He always played smart shots. Jack also played to his strengths. If he had weaknesses on certain days, he played away from them. He also had great visualization skills and wrote about this extensively. He had a special way of managing his time. Before the season started, Jack would always travel to see his teacher, Jack Grout, in Florida, and he began those sessions as if he were a beginner. That meant Mr. Grout took Nicklaus through every aspect of his golf swing and short game, from how tightly he gripped the club to how he placed his hands on the clubs. Mr. Grout would check to see how he started the club back, the full backswing, and the position at the top. Grout would work with him on his angles at setup to the position where Jack finished his swing. Very few people worked full time with a teacher then, but now we see just about every top tour player working full time with a coach. Jack also kept his golf in perspective and kept a great family life that included raising five children. Managing also means preparing the body through exercise and diet to be totally prepared for a tournament. Many more serious golfers are paying attention to stretching and overall physical fitness. *The management part of the game focuses on your lifestyle*, and it is a huge part of being a successful player.

## THE MENTAL GAME

This is how you handle the mental and emotional aspects of golf, and it determines your ability to take your range game to the golf course. Developing firm control of your mind and your emotions helps you play within yourself, frees your mind of extraneous thoughts and doubts, lets you concentrate on playing the game, and helps you perform more consistently to the level of your talent, especially in pressure situations.

I have seen numerous players on the range with beautiful golf swings.

They were good chippers, pitched the ball well, and putted great, but when they got into a golf tournament they could not play. They could not make the toughest walk in golf, *the one from the range to the first tee*. The reason is that they got too nervous, they froze, and they could not control their emotions. They just did not have it mentally to play the game. Other parts of the mental game are focus, concentration, breathing techniques, playing at your best intensity level, and visualization techniques needed to play shots on the course. These are also tremendously important. In fact, if you ask a tour professional what the most important part of the game is, they would say the mental game. When you ask them the percentage of importance to their total game, they might say 80 to 90 percent. The only problem with that is the tour players are already great in the other areas. For this reason, a tour player is not really the best person to ask. However, the ability to focus, commit, visualize, relax, and believe are perhaps the most important keys to many golf swings.

When I looked at myself as a player and as a young instructor, I saw those four components. A tour player will be very good in at least three of those four areas. I believe it is possible to compete on the PGA Tour and not be strong in one of these four components. However, you have to be very good in three areas. The greatest players are, of course, very good at all four areas.

Those four areas give me a framework through which to look at the entire game and analyze where I will start with each individual student during a lesson. When we look at most amateurs, the long game and the short game usually constitute the biggest piece we do as teachers. However, total game teachers also have to have a good grasp of sports psychology and fitness training for golf. The bottom line is that great teaching ideas last. Good golf takes time, and attention to the essentials of the game. Everyone is different, and a good teacher must adjust to the student in front of them. *A system makes it possible.*

## A TURNING POINT IN MY TEACHING

An injury incident likely changed how I improved my teaching skills and influenced how I have run my golf schools to this day. It happened when I developed tennis elbow one summer while I was still the teaching professional at Westchester Country Club in New York. I went to two different doctors in Westchester County, where the second doctor gave me cortisone injections on two occasions. Still the pain persisted. Playing in the New York Open at the famed Bethpage Black, I hit a seven-iron at the par-3 fourteenth hole. A lightning bolt went up my arm, I went to the ground. The pain in my right elbow was off the charts, and I had to walk in off the course. At this point I decided to call Dr. James Nicholas, a member of Westchester Country Club and the foremost orthopedic doctor in America. A wing at Lenox Hill Hospital is now named for this great man, who was a pioneer in sports medicine. Anyway, I took a chance that Dr. Nicholas might see me, hoping the one lesson I had given him had helped his game. Luckily he said yes, and I drove down to New York City for my appointment. It was this appointment that changed everything for me in teaching.

The professionalism I witnessed on this day stunned me. I was greeted by a professional staffer when I arrived and sat down in a beautiful waiting area. Dr. Nicholas soon opened a door and asked me to come in. We sat down. Then he looked directly into my eyes and asked me to tell him exactly what I was feeling and how I had been treating it. He left no stone unturned, and then held my arm, moving it and prodding it as I gave him feedback as to how it felt. Next he went to a full-size skeleton and pulled off the right arm. He proceeded in excruciating detail to explain exactly what had happened to my elbow and how "we" would fix it. Then he showed me two specific exercises and wrote out notes for me to take upstairs to a therapy room. I was guided by another staffer to the elevator and went up to the appropriate level. There I gave the doctor's notes to another very professional staff person, who knew exactly what to do. I followed her to a therapist, who took the notes and then took me systematically through each exercise, as well as several that Dr. Nicholas had not shown me.

I happened to notice many other patients working with Dr. Nicholas's therapists. We were all working on drills and exercises he had recommended. I realized immediately that this allowed Dr. Nicholas to see many more patients because he had a superqualified staff and supertrained therapists to carry out his prescribed treatments.

It was, and remains, the most professional operation I have ever seen. Within one month my right elbow was tremendously improved. Within two months I was totally healthy. I have never had another problem, ever, with either elbow.

I will never forget that visit to Dr. Nicholas, and this is precisely how you should approach your lessons. Make certain you understand exactly what you are doing incorrectly and then get a detailed action plan to make the necessary changes.

We teach the beginner and weekend player much differently from the advanced player. I believe that at level one you need to focus more on ball contact training and educating the hands. So we spend much more time on the hands and arms. That means lots of small swings and small shots. Most beginners and the infrequent player tend to sway and move too much. We generally teach a very quiet and steady head position. We teach the downward strike and the flat left wrist position in detail for as long as it takes.

The vast majority of golfers are in the intermediate category. I believe they need to learn more awareness of what the body does. I teach them body pivot moves and coordinating the arms and hands with the body. I also believe they need to learn an inside track to the ball. To hit with power and from the inside, it is imperative to teach a correct weight shift. There has to be a sequence from the top of the swing down to impact. To do this, I teach another McLean fundamental. That is, golf is similar to other ball-and-stick sports in that the body sequence is a *simple shift, rotate, and hit action.* This corresponds to other sports many people have played like tennis, baseball, racquetball, and also even chopping down a tree. If you played these types of sports or could throw a rock far into a lake, you have experienced the feel we are looking for in golf. That is not true with everyone; in fact, we have a lot of people who played soccer, so of course they did not use their hands and arms. I find it much more difficult to teach someone who has never played sports involving throwing or hitting. A lot of my teaching involves natural athletic moves. Notice I say *natural athletic.* *Natural* is a very bad word to use as a teacher, because natural is only what you do easily. It doesn't mean good, it means it is a habit, *but a natural "athletic" move means it corresponds to something that works in sports.*

This first means there is a loading action on the backswing, which can also be described as a slight move to the side, a coil, or a move behind the ball. Going forward, there is a lateral shifting action from the back leg to the front leg, and there also is a rotary motion of the body. If we're talking about a throwing action, it is basically the same move. You load or shift weight back (depending on how far you intend to throw), then you step toward your target, turn toward the target, and throw. That is the same sequence we try to teach people in more advanced golf. So obviously we teach a *two-pivot point swing.* I do not believe you swing around a stationary post, your spine, or a single pivot point, unless you are hitting low trajectory shots, shorter iron shots, or shots around the green. There is no question that you can hit shots with no weight transfer, but for full shots it has many disadvantages, which I will continue to point out.

*Another key fundamental of the McLean System*: Learning the proper body sequence means you can more easily learn one of the most difficult things we have to teach in golf: to hit the ball straight, the clubhead must approach from inside the target line. A swing that starts forward with the lower body (or lower center) and not the upper body or the hands has a much greater chance to facilitate an inside attack track to the ball.

For the advanced player we move to the third level, and here we often teach more of the big muscle action and in much greater depth. You probably have heard of the "big muscle swing." I first clearly learned this concept from Ken Venturi and soon thereafter from Jimmy Ballard. Advanced instruction means that your body center is initiating and the club is responding. The big muscles of the body are the shoulders, torso, and legs. They will dominate and lead. At all of our schools, in my opening presentation I separate the golf swing into two basic movements: *what the body does, and then what the club does.*

---

**Yet another key idea of the McLean System is to immediately divide the golf swing into two distinct parts. What you do with your body will definitely influence what the club does, and what you do with the club will absolutely influence what your body does. And according to each individual person, that can vary. When I am on the tour, or when tour players come to our facility, this is what most of them devote their time to. Another interesting point is that when I look at the body, I look at two centers:**

1.  **Lower center, referred to as your true center of gravity, which is located at about the belt buckle just below your belly button; also can be referred to as the body core.**
2.  **Upper center, the point at your sternum.**

**The two centers are not lined up exactly at address for normal full shots, and they do not move the same way during the swing. As I look at what the body**

---

does in the golf swing, I look very closely at what you do with your two centers. At address, for long shots we find that the upper center starts slightly behind the lower center, which means your spine angle is tilted slightly away from the target (we'll discuss this more in reference to set and setup), and it changes from short irons to your driver. You have the most tilt with the driver when the ball is more forward in your stance and also teed up. These body angles become critical to the more advanced golfer. So the better players, once they train their hands and arms, usually no longer focus as much attention on hand and arm actions. In fact, they often try to eliminate or take out conscious manipulation with the hands. They are playing more with passive hands on their routine shots. Ben Hogan wrote eloquently about this in his book *Five Lessons* and also in *Power Golf.* Jack Nicklaus wrote about it in *Golf My Way.* Jimmy Ballard said two particularly great lines: "Bad golf is played from the elbows down" and "The dog wags the tail." The concept of body control is the more advanced explanation of what the top players are trying to do. The club and hands are more responsive; they are not initiating. The top player is not consciously hitting with the hand and arms, as we see done by so many amateur golfers. They do not put a lot of energy in the hands.

Now remember—in the earlier phases of golf it is critical to train the hands, and we must do a lot of work in this area. As we get into more advanced golf we are going to a more automatic style of playing. I often describe it as only a mild conscious thought of winding and unwinding of the body, with minimal use of the hands.

When I do the opening presentations at my schools, I look at my students and ask them this question: "What is your body doing in the golf swing?" I usually get a blank stare from all of them. *This tells me most people have not thought of what they want their body to do in the swing.* That is probably because so much teaching has been done with hands and arms. To me, you must understand that the body movements are crucial to becoming a better player.

I always give a brief synopsis on body movements, and I try to assure people of one simple golf truth: as you coil up (wind up) there are only a few things that can go wrong. It is usually one of five or six moves that the average golfer makes improperly. I will be covering those Death Moves in both the back and forward swings.

## CORRIDORS OF SUCCESS

That leads me to perhaps the most unique key piece of the McLean System, the Corridors of Success and probably the defining piece of my eight-step analysis concept. **This element of the McLean System fully separates us from all the pure method instructors. They teach everyone their "perfect swing"; we teach within corridors.** I firmly believe that there are not exact positions in the golf swing but instead an acceptable range. The Eight-Step System does not involve eight exact perfect positions. In fact, throughout the golf swing there are some wide areas for you to swing the golf club, which I refer to as safety zones, corridors, or parameters. This allows all my instructors more freedom to use their own imagination and ideas to improve students. For example, they might

The backswing safety zone (widest) and the downswing safety zone (narrowest).

suggest that one student stay centered in the backswing, then with the very next student they will recommend extra lateral movement to perhaps free them up or make a much stronger coil behind the ball. Both lessons would get the student in the corridor. If you look on the PGA Tour right now or go through the history of golf, anyone who has seriously studied videotape and the game of golf must come to the conclusion that there are many ways to swing the golf club. There are fewer ways to move your body, but surely where the club goes on the backswing has been highly overrated by many teachers with many methods and systems.

Strict method teachers give the same lesson to each new student. They do not believe in Corridors of Success or variance from their perfect methods. They arrive at the range at 8 a.m. and give the same lesson from dawn to dusk. They get very good at their presentation and can deftly answer any question. The problem is they have limited research knowledge and simply close their minds to the many other ways to successfully play the game. In my mind, that has really hurt some young junior golfers by taking away their natural gifts. For example, trying to have them swing the club up on someone's image of a plane line is usually a mistake (that plane line depends on where each instructor puts the camera—and believe me, it could be anywhere). I want people to understand that there is no line going back, no perfect line, and whatever that line is, the downswing plane will be different. In truth, it is the downswing plane that is critical. Taking the club away on some perfect line is in no way going to make you a great ball striker. However, if you have a serious swing error and get out of the Corridor of Success on the backswing, we will change you. I do this because there are certain things you can do in your backswing that will definitely kill you. Remember—your backswing takes about four-fifths of a second, and your downswing takes about one-fifth of a second. So you have quite a bit of time to place the club into a solid position or, on the other hand, to do some negative move on your backswing, while then you have *just a fraction of that time to fix it on the downswing.* If you roll the clubface open on the backswing in that four-fifths of a second time slot, you now have only one-fifth of a second to square the clubface on the downswing. Things are happening a lot faster on the move forward, so that is one reason the backswing is important. A lot of amateurs (70 to 80 percent of the people who come to our schools) have either a very poor grip or a poor move away from the golf ball where they open the clubface. They are dead in the water. From a poor start and then a bad position at the top, they have to throw the golf club with the hands. Because they started outside acceptable corridors, they set themselves up for a series of catch-up moves. Firing the hands from the top is the only way they can square it up at impact. So the backswing actually did kill them; it was the Death Move in the backswing that caused them to make a very poor move from the top. This leads me to the next part of our system.

## TEACHING IN SEQUENCE

I teach golf in a sequence. *By that I mean we use a building block approach.* It is also called "first things first," something Jackie Burke beat into my psyche. To me, good teaching comes from a step-by-step approach, like a detective. I want to see what mistakes happened first. That mistake may cause a larger error later in the swing that may be much more obvious. Perhaps you lifted up through impact, or broke down coming in to impact, or you fell back on your right leg coming into the golf ball. These almost always result from a mistake you made earlier. Great training in the top business operations happens the same way. They use a step-by-step approach to reach maximum efficiency. My system involves looking at the swing in eight steps or eight positions or eight stages. All of my teachers are trained to check the swing in an orderly fashion. Now you can do the same. We are going to view the golf swing in total, and hopefully you will look at your golf swing through these different positions to see what may be going wrong in your swing. By correcting things in a sequence, you have a chance to make a quantum leap in your golf game. Beyond the sequential look at your swing, this book most importantly provides the other building blocks to golf improvement.

## THE THREE McLEAN RULES TO IMPROVEMENT

When I work with a player, I make sure he or she follows the Three McLean Rules to Improvement. Every Jim McLean instructor is taught to diligently use the Three Rules for every lesson. Here they are:

1. You must know **what you are doing right now.** That means not what you think you are doing, or what you hope you are doing, not what you were doing five years ago, or what you hope to do next year, but actually what is happening right now. That is why the video computer analysis we do is so important. You can do the same at your house or at the range with your video.

2. What should you be doing **instead** of what you are doing right now? That means you have to have a clear picture of what needs to be happening as opposed to what you are doing.

3. Finally, you must know **how** to make the change. That's where this book comes in or where a good teacher becomes important.

Most golfers worldwide go to their driving range in a very huge dilemma: They do not know what they are doing, plus they do not know what they should be doing. This leads them to listening to just about anybody walking up and down the range. That person walking up and down the range may be a ten-handicap or fifteen-handicap golfer. What is he going to tell you? Probably he will tell you what he is working on with his swing, or what he read recently in a magazine, or what he saw on the Golf Channel, or some cliché to try to help you. This cliché unquestionably works for somebody at some time. However, the chance of that idea being correct for you is very small. That is because what you are doing and what they are doing is most likely not the same thing. A lot of things happen in a golf swing, and it takes a pretty good eye to pick out what really is the cause of the problem.

"How to make the change" is the final step to improvement. This is where a top teacher, a top instructional video, or a top instructional manual will lead you down the proper path. At our schools we say there are **four basic ways to learn a new swing mechanic:**

1. Read or be told what to do (*verbal*).
2. See or copy a model (*visual*).
3. Have a teacher move you into position; you "feel" the changes (*kinesthetic*).
4. Do a drill that focuses on the swing error and corrects the problem (*drill*).

## THE JIM McLEAN THEORY OF ELIMINATION— A BREAKTHROUGH CONCEPT

*A McLean Teaching Fundamental.* The more an instructor can break down the movement of the body and the club into separate elements, the clearer the student's understanding of the Eight-Step Swing. Furthermore, through repetition of isolated movements, it's possible to accelerate the learning process.

Here are some simple ideas I have long preached on the general topic of "elimination and isolation for improvement." Follow this system in sequence, and you'll quickly break down any learning impairments that have previously blocked you from reaching your true golfing potential. It has worked well for me.

1. **Eliminate the Course.** Take away the course. Get away from playing golf on the course. Instead, go to the driving range and concentrate

on swing tempo and swing position improvements (relative to the eight steps). Going to the range is a major stress reducer. Your golf muscles will be less tense, thereby enabling you to swing better.

2. **Eliminate the Range.** Take away the range. If you're not getting good results on the range, practice hitting balls into a driving net. This effectively eliminates ball flight anxiety. Without this deterrent, you will focus much more on the swing.

3. **Eliminate the Hit.** Take away the ball. In other words, focus solely on the swing. Now that the "hit impulse" is removed, you'll stop trying too hard and swinging too fast.

4. **Eliminate Bad Swings.** Take away the club. That leaves just the arms, legs, and body to do the swinging. Without the club, body awareness further improves.

5. **Eliminate Bad Motion.** Take away the arms. Fold your arms onto your chest, and work on just footwork and body motion until you get it right.

Most golfers look for most of their improvement through the long game. However, it is the entire package that makes a complete player. As a teacher and coach I try to touch on all facets of the game. As a player you need to look at all the things that can help you achieve golf success.

I simply keep "eliminating" until the student makes improved movements and understands exactly what should be done. Once that is accomplished, we move on.

Many times a clear picture of the swing will allow you to eliminate any unnecessary actions in your technique. So, if you and your instructor can isolate any faulty movements and work together on a groove with only those choice steps that fall within the Corridors of Success, you will soon evolve into a very efficient swinger. Once you accomplish that goal, you are on your way to being a true player. You'll have a dependable swing that you can produce under pressure.

All good players pay their dues at the range.

The Jim McLean Theory of Elimination: Hitting into a net takes away the anxiety about where the ball goes. This can be very productive when you are making a change in your swing.

By removing the ball, the golfer
can often accelerate the learning process.

Making correct motions without
a club enhances body awareness.

## BECOMING A PLAYER

In golf swings there are few iron-clad rules. Here are several items a teacher must evaluate with each student:

> *Natural talents*
> *Intuitive skills*
> *Belief in their swing*
> *Producing under pressure*
> *Do they have a golf swing they can repeat?*

## An offbeat idea from Lee Trevino

Lee Trevino told me that the problem with the mythical perfect backswing is that any slight mistake anywhere in the downswing would result in a bad shot. Anything other than absolutely perfect was bad. That's why he felt his odd backswing, which included a loop that put him "in the slot" time after time, was an advantage. It was, to me, a very different way to think of the perfect backswing. It is also something I have learned from talking with truly great players; they think differently from others. He knew his swing and relied on his signature move at the top, something he could always rely on. Swings that have a "move" seem to be easier to repeat. Snead, Hogan, Trevino, Nicklaus—all had individual characteristics at the top. If Jack Nicklaus had changed his so-called flying right arm/elbow at the top, what do you think would have happened? Would a perfect backswing have helped him? There are many modern teachers who, if given a chance, would answer in the affirmative and who would have changed Jack's backswing. Now that is a scary thought. I'm sure we would never have known Jack Nicklaus, who may have been the greatest driver and long iron player in golf history, not to mention the greatest player of the 20th century.

Teaching the swing through steps or positions is not new, as I've already emphasized. My eight steps or checkpoint positions are different because of the parameters, or Corridors of Success, that I believe allow for necessary individualism.

Methods that tightly standardize the golf swing are dangerous because few golfers can perform all the movements and swing positions of the model. Method teachers who use rigid guidelines close their minds and eyes to other swing actions and body movements that can, and in fact, do work.

Hitting "every" shot according to a rigid method for swinging the club and going through a checklist usually makes playing under pressure tremendously more difficult for almost every golfer. My own shortcomings in this area led me to understand that many things can be overdone, some of the oldest accepted axioms were incorrect, and some teaching adages such as "hit late" had to be reevaluated. It is possible to have too much lag in your swing.

> **At an early stage of development, especially with youngsters, staying steady and delaying the hit can be taught very successfully. However, using the arms and hands to create lag is usually only a stage of development. At a later advanced stage, remaining motionless, staying absolutely centered (the stationary post), and continuously working on lag not only can become dangerous but can promote Death Positions.**
>
> **The example above shows that some positions, when practiced to an extreme, can cause tremendous damage even to highly skilled athletes and, in the end, make the game much harder indeed.**

Position instruction, when done right, breaking the swing into component parts or teaching through steps, is a tremendous accelerator to the learning process. Teaching this way is especially good for isolating problems and correcting the fault. Yet positions have limitations.

When swing mechanics become the entire focal point of the teacher, the student ceases to become a skilled player. Instead, he or she becomes a confused, tense, robotic golfer. Most people reading this book have likely witnessed someone who has flamed out on scientific swing mechanics.

When a certain position or set of positions becomes the goal, the act of swinging and being an athlete often gets lost in the details. We need to remember that a true swinging action produces the consistency we all desire. I maintain that Corridors of Success allow individual differences and individual talent to exist within the eight steps. This freedom will allow extremely talented golfers to do it their way.

Remember that wherever you learn golf, including from me, ideas or fundamentals are based on what we have seen, learned, or experienced. Science tells us that today's laws of physics may be proved wrong tomorrow. So there is no system that may not be improved down the road.

In my opinion and my experience, teaching through a series of steps has exceptional instructional value. Yet, these steps, or positions, have limitations. To quote Harvey Penick, "Take some of the medicine, but don't swallow the whole bottle."

Finally, I always go back to my 25 Percent Theory. Practice the whole game. Remember—it is not just the swing. Realize we are playing the game of golf consisting of these four areas. Find out what part of the game you need to really work at. It may not be the long game.

# 3

# DEATH MOVES

*Extreme Swing Errors Outside the Corridors of Success*

The following are what I label Death Moves. They are actions and positions in the golf swing that are so far from ideal that—if not changed—they will doom you to poor shots forever. With violations of swing fundamentals this dramatic, there is simply no compromise. A radical and immediate change of habit is required. All of my teachers study and understand Death Moves!

If you come to my schools with one of these mistakes, you will definitely be taught how to fix it, and you will leave with a complete understanding of why something is a Death Move and how to eliminate it. Simply put, do not allow any of the following swing killers to ruin your chances of ever playing the game well.

1. Freezing over the ball with no waggle and/or ignition movement, causing excessive tension to build up at setup before starting the club away from the ball.

2. Leaving the majority of your weight on your left leg on the backswing to such a degree that the left leg becomes the pivot point, creating a classic reverse pivot. The head shifts toward the target, and the hips twist on the left leg.

3. Overextending or "disconnecting" the left arm from the upper torso during the backswing. This sometimes comes from golfers trying to create "width."

4. Rolling your hands over dramatically in a clockwise direction during the take-away. This opens the clubface and causes the club to feel heavy, as it is now severely out of balance. The clubface points up toward the sky. The clubshaft is severely laid off and nearly horizontal to the ground.

5. Too little hip turn combined with no weight shift. This causes a short shoulder turn and no power. Some teachers and some golfers have mistaken lower body resistance to mean no hip turn or over-restricted lower body motion.

6. Turning the clubface into an extremely shut position during the backswing, causing severe hooks and/or extra-low trajectory. Many times a closed clubface in the take-away will not kill you, but if you always hook and pull shots, it needs to be changed. We will work on getting your clubface square, or what feels very open.

7. Turning the clubface into an extremely open position at the top of the backswing. The Number One mistake we see at our golf schools is the student who turns the clubface wide open at the top. It is a

huge swing killer and one of the most common Death Moves. We change your backswing position immediately.

8. Right arm folding immediately into the body, meaning that the right elbow attaches to the body and narrows the arc of the backswing. Most players will have a huge power loss. For the golfer who needs more power, the tucked right elbow and super narrow backswing is death.

9. Allowing the clubshaft to tip forward in a steep orientation on the downswing. A devastating move. I see this move quite regularly. The backswing is slightly flat, and then the golfer re-routes the wrists at the top, causing the shaft to move into a steep angle of attack. This is the exact opposite from the move most pros use.

10. Dropping the clubshaft under the right arm as you start the downswing, causing the angle of attack to be too shallow and from the inside. Although solid shots can occasionally be hit from this position, mostly thin, fat, pushed, or badly hooked shots result. This usually happens with club professionals or low-handicap golfers who appear to have good-looking swings but who shoot high scores in tournaments or have wild mis-hits. It's a massive swing mistake.

11. The body sliding or drifting past the ball on the forward swing. This is a high-handicap mistake. Way too much body slashing.

12. Dramatic lifting or dipping in the backswing. This can happen to people with injuries or bad backs. Very understandable, but unfortunately also a terrible golf move.

13. Having weight on toes at setup. Also, during the backswing, letting the weight shift to the toe of the back foot. If you notice weight moving onto your back toe area in the backswing, you'll know why you're inconsistent. It is not an acceptable mistake. Change it immediately.

14. Making a fast move away from the ball with the hands. Causes a "fake" turn that lacks loading on the right side, kills timing, and produces a powerless move to the ball.

15. Allowing the head to move in front of the ball while hitting a driver off a tee. Good players leave the head six to ten inches behind the ball at impact on their driver swing. No tour player slides the head past the position where the head was at address. So don't do it!

16. Spinning the back foot at the start of the downswing rather than shifting the lower body to the left. Because the shoulders open too soon, an ineffective extreme outside-in swing path results, producing a classic slice or pull.

17. Throwing the club from the top of the backswing with the hands without initiating the downswing with a lower body shift. Remember— there is a sequence to any hitting or throwing motion that works properly. "Casting" is a classic high-handicapper Death Move.

18. Moving the left heel backwards as the downswing begins, causing a weak reverse weight shift before impact. I see so many high-handicappers start the downswing by shifting the left heel away from the target. The left hip backs away in response, and the golfer swipes across the ball.

19. Disconnecting the upper left arm from the left side of the chest, breaking down the most important body connection in the swing, which the best players maintain through the impact zone, while poor players' left arms form a "chicken wing" or a wiping action across the ball. The clubshaft usually swings well under the plane.

20. Letting the left wrist break down at impact—perhaps the Number One Death Move. The right arm and clubshaft form a straight line at impact. This is a very common high-handicapper mistake.

21. Allowing the clubhead to travel inside out past impact and the club-shaft to rise vertically skyward. This Death Move causes massive hooks and pulls. The clubshaft has traveled far above the plane after impact. This is a more common Death Move than most people realize. You will hit the ball all over the golf course, because after enough

vicious hooks, you'll eventually perfect a block out to right field. There is no way to be an effective ball striker with this swing path.

## CORRECTING DEATH MOVES

First, you must clearly understand that one or more current swing actions are killing your chances of hitting quality golf shots. So identify your Death Moves. Next, you need to correct the mistake with an improved golf motion. To do this, I ask you to make hundreds of small swings learning the correct move. Do this without hitting balls. Learn a proper practice swing, and groove it. Then, when you begin striking balls, do it with very small swings at low swing speeds. This will be the way to accelerate true improvement. Do not attempt to bypass the repetition phase of swing change. Be patient, and you will be rewarded.

**4**

# THE SET

*The Unique Way JMGS Teaches the Setup*

*"Golf is 40 percent setup."*

—JACK NICKLAUS

I often refer to the address routine as the set instead of the setup. To me, it's

part of correct technique in much the same way a sprinter's position in

the blocks is part of running the fastest time. When players have gone

through their pre-shot routine properly, they know the shot they want to

hit and the ball flight they desire. But these decisions can be carried out

only if the players get set to the ball in a manner that suits the shot.

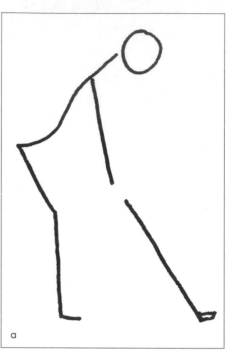

a. Cupped lower back: This promotes tension and tightness. It can also be from a weak back.

b. Rounded back is the most common high handicap problem. This is slumped over with a weak back and stomach.

c. Robot setup: The tailbone to the top of the head in a perfect line. This causes too much knee flex and tension in the shoulders and neck.

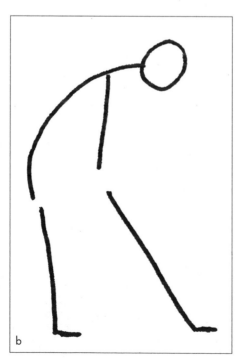

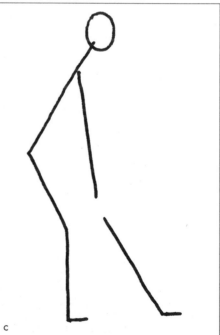

*Setup basics:* At address, you bend forward from the hip girdles with your knees flexed and "live tension" in your legs. Both feet are flat on the ground, with the inside muscles of the legs and feet activated, and your weight is equally distributed on the entire foot, from the ball of each foot back to the heel. Usually (from the view facing the target), the hips are square to the target line, with the hip "girdles" pushed to the rear so that a straight line down from the bottom of the spine hits four to eight inches behind the heels. The clubhead is normally in line with the hands, or within the allowable Corridor of Success.

Check this in a mirror. Ideally, the butt of the club points between your navel and the crease of your slacks. Deviating from this configuration is not recommended. As long as you keep your hands and the club's handle between your body center and the crease of your slacks, you are within the acceptable parameters.

> **Setup is not a step. Rather, it is positioning your body and club into a great golfer's address.**

*How to see the correct position:* As you look down at the ball, the club's shaft will appear to lean toward the target, when in fact it is not.

## SET YOUR BODY "PARALLEL LEFT" (BUT NOT REALLY)

An excellent starting point for the amateur golfer is to set up *parallel* to the ball-to-target line. I often use the popular image of railroad tracks to get this point across. The ball-to-target line is the outside rail, and the inside rail is the line the player uses to set the body alignments. This mental picture is widely used because it is virtually foolproof, and it presents a vividly clear mental picture that all students can easily relate to.

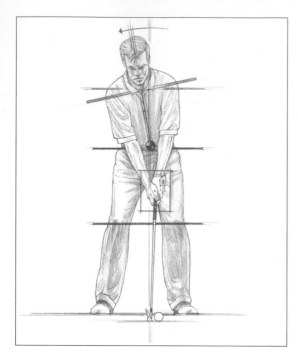

**Top left:** Spine tilt corridor and body angles. The perfect model setup. Remember—I adjust many students to a setup position that varies from this so-called perfect position. Many great players set up off these lines. The goal is to hit long straight shots.

**Top right:** Practice setup for the driver. Notice the shaft leaning slightly back.

**Bottom:** Your body should line up parallel to the target line, with your shoulders slightly open to the target.

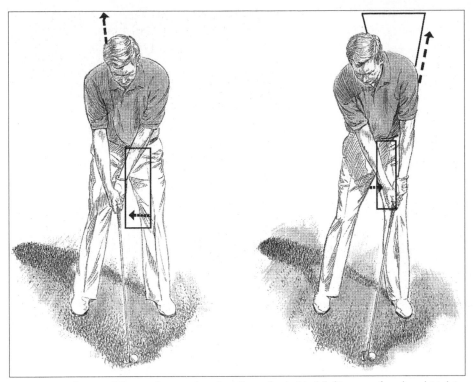

In setting up, be careful not to let your hands drift too far behind (left), or too far ahead (right). The Corridor of Success is identified above and subsequent photos.

Along that inside rail, students should set their eyes, shoulders, hips, knees, forearms, and feet. Minor adjustments to this initial parallel model can be made with time. To simplify it, remember that the arms, which connect to the club, are attached to the shoulders. Therefore, the alignment of the shoulders is most critical of all. Because the right hand is farther away from the body than the left, your shoulder line will be set slightly left of the inside rail. This is natural and also correct. I set the shoulders closed for students only when trying to increase the inside attack approach. It is clear that the great ball hitters set the upper body parallel to the target line, or significantly more open. Interestingly, some of the great tour players whom I've studied closely set up closed with the lower body and open with the upper body—especially with the longer clubs.

If you take a serious look at players on all the major tours, you will see a surprising difference in their setup alignments, similar to the differences we see at the top of the backswing. A significant number of top players will be set up "off the line." That means they are aimed either open or closed. Their stances are not perfectly parallel like the model swing. As with many things in golf, players change and adjust to get the desired ball flight characteristics. Players with open stances include Jack Nicklaus, Lee Trevino, Fred Couples, Angel Cabrera, and most players who fade the ball. Most "open stance players" will drop or loop the club to the inside on the downswing and into a great Step Five delivery position. When a better player is getting too steep on the downswing, an easy fix is to "open them up." Then I have them hit shots out to right field until they get the "feel" of the more shallow and inside motion. Others like Sam Snead, Rocco Mediate, and Jesper Parnevick set up quite closed. This is an alignment I often use with higher-handicap golfers to help them swing from the inside. It tends to promote a draw.

Keep in mind that different golf course situations require different stances. The fact is that you take a new stance for almost every shot you hit on the course (a huge difference from standing on the flat range). So remember—the square stance is a very good model, and we teach this all the time at my schools. However, we also teach adjustments, and how you can self-correct during a round when things just are not working. Since we don't play golf off a flat surface and with zero wind, that in itself logically requires adjustments. Beyond that, some students will do much better setting "off the line," just like some of the best players in the world.

## ONE BALL POSITION FOR EVERY SHOT? NO WAY!

Think of a fairway bunker shot, a shot into a forty-miles-per-hour wind, hitting off a downslope, hitting off a severe side hill lie, hitting a driver over a tree to cut the dogleg, or hooking a three-wood around a severe dogleg.

This is the obvious rebuttal to advocates of the "one-ball-position-for-every-shot" theory. To me, it is absolutely ludicrous to think you can play all shots from one position in your stance. Not only is most every shot you hit on the golf course from a different lie, often you have particular wind conditions and pin locations that require you to hit a low shot, high shot, draw, hook, fade, or slice. Instead of changing your entire swing and weight distribution for every shot, simply change the ball position. To hit different shots requires that you change something. To me, it is obvious that the easiest change is *ball position*.

Let's have a reality check. To hit a short iron on a pure "tour pro" trajectory—that is, relatively low with maximum backspin—will require a different striking action from a drive hit off a tee from flat ground. Of course, you could play that short iron off your left heel or instep, as one-ball-position advocates suggest. But then you'd also have to put 70 percent of your weight on your forward foot at address, set up with your hands well ahead of the ball, increase your grip pressure, make a huge lateral move into the ball on the downswing, concentrate extra hard on keeping your hands way ahead of the clubhead in the hitting area, and drive the clubhead low through and well past the ball.

Wouldn't you rather just move the ball back in your stance and make a shorter, firmer version of your normal swing to hit this shot? I believe you would, and you should.

On paper, to a theorist, playing the ball from one position for all shots may seem like a good idea. To an accomplished player, it's a joke. Even if the rare tour player tells you that they play the ball from the same point in their stance on every shot, don't believe it. *It is a super simple idea for a super simple mind. It might sound good at first, but you take a new stance every time you set up to an odd lie.* Typical pros have played golf almost their entire lives and therefore must be making automatic adjustments to different playing circumstances. If these adjustments are second nature to you as well, you can go right on thinking you play every shot from the same spot. Just don't start

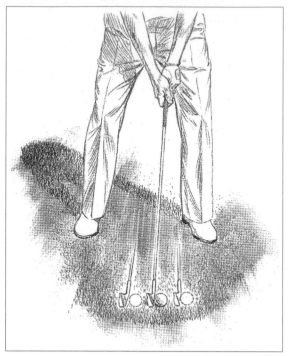

Ball position varies from shot to shot, depending upon endless variables.

doing it. Ball position moves from the center of your stance for wedges, up to the left heel for the driver. The width and positioning of stance make exact positioning off any part of the body impractical.

## DISTANCE FROM THE BALL

Here I'm talking about the space between your hands and your body. As with much of golf, there is no perfect answer, but there are some excellent clues. For example, your hands are farther from your body with the driver than with any other club. Teachers who say that the hands stay in one location for all clubs don't know what they are talking about.

It is another example of a seemingly simple answer to the golf swing that does not work. *"Fourteen different golf clubs, fourteen different lie angles, fourteen different lengths, fourteen different weights, fourteen different stances . . . In reality, on the golf course, a thousand different stances."* As each of your clubs increases in length and each lie angle is progressively flatter, the hands move farther from the body. Therefore, the old adage that all clubs are a "hand's width" from the body is not correct.

The other mistake I often hear is "You can't stand too close to the ball." I've seen golf's greatest drivers all with wide spacing between the hands and the body. However, with the short irons, these same players will have the hands much closer in. One easy way to establish the proper distance from the ball is at setup. Before placing the club on the ground, hold the club parallel to the ground and directly in front of your body. Relax your arms and measure the distance from the butt end of the club to your belt buckle. Then simply maintain this distance as you lower the club behind the ball. You'll be pleasantly surprised how easily this works.

Generally, tall golfers will use longer shafts and have more upright lie angles. Shorter golfers will have standard-length clubs but flatter lie angles. That flat lie angle will usually cause the butt end of the grip to be farther away from the body.

Remember that some people have very long arms and fingers, while others have short arms and small hands. That's why a teacher must be able to adjust to the student, especially at setup. There must be a range to work within. It is another clear reason why methods will not work. You cannot teach the same setup spacing for every student. It simply will not work.

## ALIGNMENT TELLS THE TALE

*Often, the harder you work on your swing, the tougher it is for you to believe that most golf shots are missed even before the swing begins.* Be that as it may, a poor shot is often the result of poor alignment in the setup. Ken Venturi always drilled home the point that golfers don't lose their swing so much as they *lose their position at address*. "They don't get out of swing," Ken would say; "they get out of position." The more I've taught, the more I agree.

Alignment is complicated by the fact that so many different body parts—the feet, knees, hips, shoulders, forearms, eyes—must be brought into position relative to the target line. Remember—the shoulders will actually be slightly more open simply because your right hand is farther away from center than the left hand. When you change just one of these factors, you exert some change on the desired ball flight. Pay attention to all alignments, and do it on a daily basis. A great tip I learned from Venturi was to actually measure your alignments and distance to the ball when you are playing your best. Then, when you are off, you can easily go back to check alignment mistakes for "your game." This is one good thing I gave Tom Kite during our years of working together. He still uses his "perfect alignment guide" almost twenty years later.

## SET UP TENSION FREE

Tension is often a by-product of poor concentration, but in the golf swing, tension threatens to undo all your preparations. ***Tension kills the golf swing***. A quick check for signs of tension is to observe the forearms, wrists, hands, shoulders, neck, and thighs. If the muscles are contracted and tensed, your swing is in trouble before it begins. Back away, breathe deeply and exhale very slowly, shake out the tension, then *reset* in a relaxed manner. Breathe in through the nose and out through the mouth. Remember to evaluate your grip pressure on a scale of one (*superlight*) to ten (*supertight*), and for normal shots, keep it right around five or under (*moderate to light*), as discussed in the previous chapter.

"Tension kills the golf swing": a quote I use almost every day. This picture shows the golfer gliding to a relaxed finish.

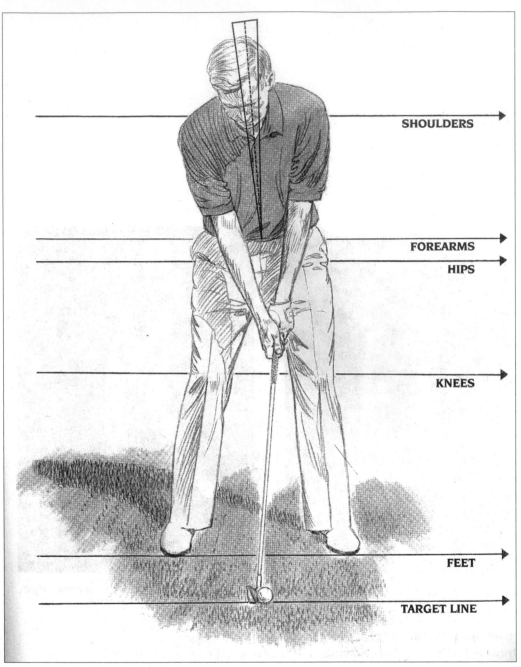

SHOULDERS

FOREARMS

HIPS

KNEES

FEET

TARGET LINE

Corridor of Success for spine tilt (between 1 degree and 15 degrees of right side bending at address).

Address (left) and impact (right) are not the same. In fact, everything is different.

Moment of truth.

## THE SETUP POSITION DOES NOT SIMULATE THE IMPACT POSITION

I'm amazed at the number of students I teach who still believe they strike the ball by returning their body to the same position they set at address. This is totally incorrect. To see the difference, thumb through some of your old golf magazines and view photographs of the pros at impact. The positions they are in do not look much like their setup positions, do they? What has happened is that everything has shifted toward the target. The weight is at least 70 percent to the left side. Most often, the head of a top ball striker drops slightly as the upper body compresses in the downswing. If you watch this closely on videotape, you might be very surprised by the most fine players who have a noticeable drop. The hands are well out in front of the address alignment. The left wrist is flat. The right heel is off the ground, and the right knee is kicking forward at the ball. The hips are turned well left, at least thirty degrees in a full swing. The shoulders should also be slightly open to the target line, with the right shoulder lower and the left shoulder higher. Clearly, not much resembles the alignments made during the setup.

As in all things, the preparatory work is often underestimated. The proper setup in golf gets you positioned for success. A poor setup is a killer. So read this chapter carefully, and underline key points for your continuing reference.

# 5

# PREPARATION AND PRESHOT ROUTINE

*How to Ensure a Good Shot Before Addressing the Ball*

Good players, and tour professionals in particular, strive to make the time between arriving at their ball and hitting the shot their most highly focused and standardized action on the golf course.

They know that all the detailed preparatory work relative to planning a shot has a direct influence on the result. If the golfer goes through a very thorough process of surveying the on-course situation and also visualizes or feels a good shot vividly before swinging, there's an excellent chance that precisely that shot will be hit.

In the case of the typical amateur, as I have already stated, most shots are missed before they are played. As a result of passivity, neglect, or ignorance, the average golfer fails to carefully evaluate such vital things as the lie, the target area, and the target line. Nor do they rehearse or visualize the swing they intend to make before addressing the ball.

Don't make the same mistakes. Instead, adhere to a set shot procedure, and it will be a prelude to success.

The following routine is not complex, but it is thorough. It is used for every shot and encompasses only that brief period (fifteen to forty-five seconds) during which you are preparing for and executing the shot. I'm one person who believes in being quick with your assessments. Coach Wooden said, "Be quick, but don't hurry." Excellent advice! Make your assessments and decisions in a timely manner. For the remainder of the time between shots, relax and have fun with the people in your group. If you make the effort to practice the pre-shot routine sequence until it is ingrained, you *will* see improvement in your play.

## PREPARATION FOR THE ROUTINE

### Procedure One: Survey

A golf course is a diverse environment full of subtleties and surprises. Whether you generally strike the ball seventy times or one hundred times per round, you should devote serious attention to the circumstances surrounding your ball—including the lie, distances, and conditions—all with an eye toward the precise results you want to achieve. Good players don't miss a thing, taking in all pertinent information. The best way to analyze all the variables is to break them down individually in the following manner:

An uneven lie will change your setup positions and body angles.

Assess all information; here, checking wind direction.

**A. Identify Your Ball.** Make sure the ball you're getting ready to hit is yours. If you hit the wrong ball in a match-play event, you automatically lose the hole. If you hit the wrong ball (except in a hazard) during a stroke-play event, you will be penalized two strokes. Smart players personalize their ball before playing by putting a distinctive mark on it with a pencil or pen. The reason: it's not out of the ordinary to be playing the same brand and number.

**B. Analyze the Lie.** Look at the slope of the land, examine the type of grass you're hitting from and the direction it grows, determine whether the grass is wet or dry, determine whether there is hardpan underneath the ball, and so on. An experienced player has learned to make judgments like these in an instant.

**C. Check the Lay of the Land.** Determine whether the stance required will have an effect on your swing or the likely flight of the ball (for

In preparing to swing, take an extra second to relax and aim the clubface.

When hitting to a blind green, it's particularly important to pick a target along the line to the hole, such as a tree in the distance.

example, a shot hit from a right-to-left slope will cause a flatter swing and make a hook likely). Make mental adjustments before you hit the shot.

**D. Check Wind Direction and Wind Speed.** Although you should determine the direction of the prevailing wind before teeing off, be careful to not be fooled by flags on greens that are still. They may be blocked by tall trees. Look at the tops of the trees to see if there is wind that will affect your shot. You can toss grass up into the air or check the ripples on nearby lakes or ponds.

**E. Identify Your Target Line.** Identifying the target line will allow you to set properly all your body alignments. Many golfers choose an intermediate target from one foot to several yards ahead of their ball, on the target line.

**F. Survey the Target Area.** Is the target area flat, sloping, hard, or soft? Check for your "exit area"—the spot where a safe shot can be played or where a missed shot can land. Generally, though not always, one side of the green is more clear of trouble or severe slopes. There are many course situations that call for a more safe play, even for the fine player. For instance, Jack Nicklaus often plays to the center of many greens and always clearly analyzes the surrounding safe spots.

**G. Determine Distance.** The tournament player must be exact and not estimate distance. He must know the distance to his desired landing area on the green, and must have "carry" yardage over bunkers or water. Such a golfer also must be aware of the depth of the green (front to back) and know the distances to different levels or severe slopes in the green.

## Procedure Two: Visualize

In your mind, picture the ball leaving and taking a specific trajectory to the target area. If you have any difficulty seeing the shot, simply ask yourself, "What am I trying to do?" Clarity is essential at this point. You must make a pure commitment to your target and have a precise idea of what type of shot you are planning to play.

Form a mental image of the swing. For some folks, this will be detailed and clear. For others, it will be automatic and sensed via "feel."

Dr. Richard Coop, with whom I have conducted some golf schools, has convinced many of the top players in the world that their preshot routine can start with a conscious cue. Your cue should be some physical act. This cue is your signal to begin focusing intensely on the situation at hand and to be able to sustain it until the shot is hit. Some, but certainly not all, golfers benefit greatly by using a conscious cue. Generally, golfers who have difficulty

A yardage pad or booklet will help you hit shots the correct distance.

with the preshot routine may be helped greatly by using a conscious act or even an audible sound. Some examples are releasing and reclosing the Velcro on a glove, tugging on the sleeve of a shirt, or removing and replacing a hat.

**Be sure to change your cue periodically. You want your cue to be a conscious act, not an unconscious habit. It is done to get you into the "ignition" mode. It causes you to say, "I am going to focus on this shot completely for the next twenty seconds."**

## Procedure Three: Relax

Stand to the rear of the ball and take a cleansing breath. Exhale twice as slowly as you inhaled. You may want to shake your arms and fingers a bit if you feel extra tension. Use these simple ideas or any other relaxation techniques to get yourself prepared to play. But remember—a relaxed body and a quiet mind are the keys to *peak* performance. Also, it is very possible to be nervous yet physically relaxed.

A conscious cue, such as releasing the Velcro on your glove (left), tugging on your shirt (center), or removing your cap (right), can be used to trigger focus prior to the preshot routine.

Promote relaxation by standing behind the ball and taking a cleansing breath.

### Procedure Four: Process Your Data

On the basis of the data, make the club selection that will give you the results you desire. It's important not to choose a club until you have produced a very vivid mental picture of the shot you intend to hit. While I'm on this subject, let me make sure to say this clearly: Don't overdo this procedure. You can make all of this preshot routine so detailed that it becomes cumbersome and impedes the flow of your play.

When I played on the golf team at the University of Houston, our coach, Dave Williams (whose teams won sixteen NCAA championships), would become livid if one of his players made too much of the pre-swing analysis. When a player used the excuse of poor yardage and/or incomplete preparation, Coach Williams would scream, "If you can play this game, you can pick any club. Just take out any club and hit the ball at the flagstick! But don't make excuses and don't be indecisive. And don't ever *look* indecisive." At first glance, this advice may seem far-fetched, but believe me, there is truth in those words. *If you can play, you can be decisive. Your preshot routine will be clear. Too much thinking is just as bad as no thinking—in fact, sometimes much worse.*

## THE ROUTINE

As you stand behind your ball and begin the move to address:

1. Make a smooth and graceful walk to the side of the ball. Generally set your alignments and take an effortless practice swing. Most top players just use a practice motion to release tension and prep themselves. You may want to make the practice swing that is an exact duplicate of the swing you intend to put on the ball. Some players will find this useful. I especially like this procedure for shots around the green.

2. Approach the ball with your eyes looking at the target. Hold the club in the right hand, step into the "golfer's box" with your right foot, and set the club behind the ball. This procedure, used by many great players, is the most natural and most logical because it ensures that you are "open," which gives you a better visual perspective of the target.

3. After setting the club down, move your feet into their correct alignment positions. Take the stance necessary for this particular shot. Venturi said you get into position in three moves: "club behind the ball, place left foot, then right foot."

4. Look intently at the target, then glance at the ball while still jockeying your feet for balance. Repeat the look-glance procedure, then go! I say, "Look to the target once, look to the target twice, set, and go"— a proven procedure I stole from the great Johnny Revolta. Watch and see how many top pro golfers instinctively use this simple preshot routine.

Know your yardages and select the correct club. Once you select your club, take a confident swing.

Make your practice swing count.

The total time for the routine is less than thirty seconds. However, the only segment that truly needs to be precise is after you actually place the clubhead behind the ball and then move your feet into their correct position. That is when I start the stopwatch. If a player takes more than ten seconds to hit the ball from that moment, I encourage him to speed up.

Good players stare at the target and stay in motion. High-handicappers do just the opposite. They stare at the ball and have no motion in the lower body. Whereas the target is the most important thing in the world to a good player, the ball is the most important thing in the world to the poor player. This mistake will cause tension and will result in poor tempo and a vast array of mis-hits. Don't make this mistake.

## REVIEW

To the proficient pro, the preshot routine is *automatic*. However, by writing out all of these minute details, I run the risk of making this process appear tedious and perhaps tension-inducing to amateurs. The fact is, you can have the greatest routine in the game but never reach your potential as a golfer if your swing technique is incorrect. With no golf game, a preshot routine is worthless. Targeting, in the end, is an interesting but not necessarily definitive subject. Visualizing can be good or bad, depending upon what you see. Intense visualizing leads some golfers to steer shots or guide the ball to the target. There is a lesser-known idea of the "body mind." This is the concept of turning off the conscious mind and letting your body hit the shot with pure muscle memory and no outcome thoughts at all.

## GOLFSPEAK: FINAL THOUGHTS ON PREPARATORY MOVES

### Body Language

Something very few people consider is body language on the golf course. Yet, positive body language is so very obvious with all top players.

I spend a lot of time with my players on this aspect of the game. It's very simple: Look like you know what you are doing! Look and act confident, and you will be amazed at the resulting inner confidence in your game.

Anyone who looks scared or looks like they don't belong will usually perform poorly. From spending time with champions, I know they have a special presence. They act, talk, and walk confidently, and they take up what I call a lot of "space."

When I played tour events I took up minimal space. I was not comfortable or confident. My body language was poor. I was getting out of everybody's way. I didn't want to be on the stage. In amateur golf I was totally different, but when I stepped onto the tour I didn't carry over the same attitude or the same assured step.

Some of this is a matter of personality. Many champions have had a low-key presence, just as there have been charismatic players who have loved performing under competitive pressure. I do know that you must have confidence in your ability. The way you move gives off a distinct impression to everyone around you. I believe that self-doubt, lack of belief, and noncommitment all show up in your facial expressions and your body actions.

A champion has a certain air and physical movement that conveys that he or she can handle all situations. It's hard to prove, but body language is important and hugely underrated. Walk, talk, and act like a champion, and over time this will have a positive effect on everything you do in golf.

## Imprinting

All of us will go to an automatic pilot response under stress or in tournament situations. When this happens you will perform according to your inner self-image. If your self-image is strong you will likely succeed. Lanny and Troy Bassham run my sports psychology program in Ft. Worth, Texas. Lanny, a former Olympic gold medalist, is adamant about the power of self-image imprinting.

All the things you constantly think about and visualize almost always come true. These images are imprints in your brain, and your brain works similarly to a computer. It stores those imprints. When you think about something or see something, a new imprint is made in your head.

Very often, certain golf situations activate an automatic response from a player based on what's been imprinted from his experiences and his attitude about those experiences. It's like pressing a button for a pre-set station on a car radio.

Visualize your target. Then let go.

Ken Venturi, through his mentoring from Nelson and Hogan, always told me that strong belief in the ability to pull off a particular shot was the most important factor in hitting a good shot. I too believe that pre-set image is so powerful that nobody can overestimate its importance. "The most beautiful technique will be ruined by a bad shot image, while a positive strong shot image can save a more flawed swing technique."

# 6

# THE EIGHT-STEP SWING

*Building Your Swing with Jim McLean's Breakthrough Framework*

**PRELUDE TO EFFECTIVE INSTRUCTION**

A good teacher is one whose students consistently get better. It's as simple as

that. In the same way, an effective swing is simply a swing that hits the ball

solidly and long with a certain pattern, with a slight fade, straight, or with a

slight draw, time after time and if necessary under pressure. If you don't think

that is true, I give you Tom Lehman, Jack Nicklaus, Sergio Garcia, Jim Furyk,

Arnold Palmer, Ryan Moore, Annika Sorenstam, Andres Romero, and Lee Trevino.

A good teacher has to possess enough broad knowledge to know what to leave alone. He has to know what makes a swing produce great golf shots, not whether that swing conforms to certain fixed ideas. Again, what are the true fundamentals of golf? What made Bruce Lietzke possibly the greatest driver on the PGA Tour for twenty-five years in a row with a swing that went inside on the backswing, had the clubface closed at the top, and had a loop over the top? What made that work? A good teacher knows and respects that the unorthodox can be correct for that person. A bad teacher doesn't, and can thus change that which is most essential for a particular player.

I give this preamble because the Eight-Step Swing is not an exact template for how a swing should look. It's a statement of principles that can be followed, with room for individual idiosyncrasies. It's a framework with flexibility.

I don't teach the Eight-Step Swing all at once. Often, I do not even mention the steps in a particular order. Rather, as I analyze a swing and also in explaining critical golf moves within small sections of the swing, I use these positions to mentally organize my approach to each individual. It improves my ability to develop a game plan tremendously.

I also use these points in the swing to key in on problems. My teaching plan then becomes much easier for each individual lesson. My game plan is to diagnose the first problem in the player's swing. Once this is identified, I analyze why it is happening and then determine how I'll attack the problem.

The concept of swinging through eight steps is way too much for the average golfer. So when I use the steps, I simply eliminate three, four, five, or more positions. Often the key positions for the average player are Steps Two, Four, Six, and Eight. Whatever positions I teach, I make sure they are crystal clear in the mind of each student. Then I teach them how to make the move to achieve a solid position. I explain, demonstrate, have them execute, then repeat, repeat, repeat.

Many advanced players can easily adapt to all the steps, if necessary. After an advanced player visualizes the steps and then carefully swings through all the positions, it's only a matter of time until it becomes routine. Soon enough, there will be no thoughts in his or her mind about swinging into or through positions that are all within an acceptable range. An advanced player can, if need be, replicate exact positions. In my system you need not attempt to master precise and exact positions in golf. Nobody has a perfect swing with every angle and body part in a model position. Trying to be perfect generally leads to overanalysis and a loss of freedom. Letting go and having freedom in your swing is a huge key to golf success.

Placing the club through certain key positions can, however, produce tremendous results. I believe that, to a significant degree, you can place the club into nearly exact positions through the backswing because "in golf time" this is very slow. I sometimes have students think, if necessary, of the backswing as a "placement situation." If you know the locations, you can, in time, achieve dramatic results. The time required is different from player to player, but it can be achieved.

From technically correct backswing positioning, coiling, and swinging the golf club within the corridors (body plus club), the chances of achieving fundamental downswing and forward swing positions are greatly enhanced.

On the other hand, I believe that the move down to the ball (to impact) cannot be guided. Rather, you need to let go, to commit forward with abandonment. Think: control back; let go forward! *Any top professional will tell you that to gain control of your shots, you will need to give up control of your swing. This may well be the ultimate paradox of golf.*

I have used the Eight-Step Swing positions in my teaching since 1986. Positions work because students understand how and what to improve. They then know what to work on when they practice alone. They have a plan when they go to the range. This gives them a huge advantage over the other golfers who go to a range with no plan and only random swing thoughts.

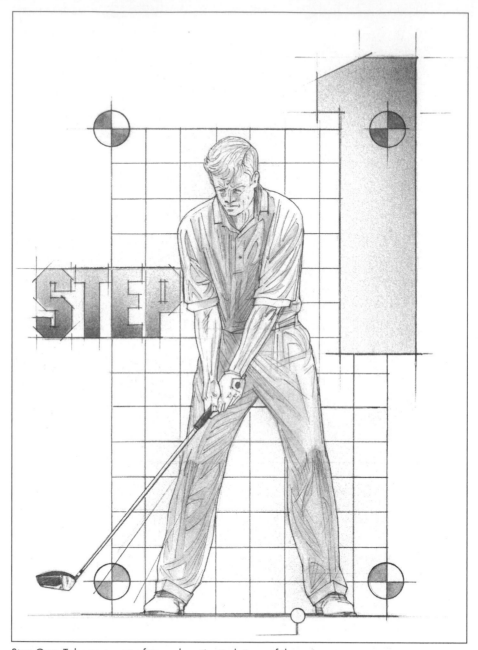

Step One: Take-away, an often underestimated stage of the swing

Step One: Target line view. The clubhead's working slightly inside and up.

## STEP ONE: THE FIRST MOVE IN THE BACKSWING

Closely watch the accomplished golfer make a smooth movement of the club away from the ball. I believe you should always strive for a smooth one-piece motion as you begin the take-away. In the next pages I will explain "one piece" in detail.

The point in the backswing when the clubhead has moved about three feet away from the ball may seem like a premature time for evaluation. Not so at all. This is Step One in a solid golf swing, and I regard this initial move as crucial. In fact, if you can master the requirements of Step One, the remainder

Step One: The drawing on the left shows the arms and hands controlling the take-away. The drawing on the right shows center (or the body) controlling the initial move away from the ball.

of the swing will fall into place more easily. If Step One is flawed, the golf swing is in a state of recovery until impact. So it is extremely important to be precise at Step One. It is the one area of the swing in which there is less room for personal preference. Therefore, strive for precision at Step One.

### The Mini "Micro" Move

*What starts the club back?* Interestingly, it should be a mini-move forward. You can take control of this vital initial movement by triggering it with a mini-move of your own choosing. I suggest you lift your right heel slightly and return that heel to the ground as a trigger, or use a slight body or hand press toward the target, but make it a very small move. With practice, your ignition move becomes totally second nature and is usually unnoticeable to the average viewer. This micro-move forward helps create a beautiful rebound or counter mini-movement back to the right (weight shift). *Therefore, the first move in the backswing is slightly forward. Another golf paradox.*

### The First Move Back

Then comes the first move back, which should be a *one-piece action*. In other words, everything together—shoulders, arms, hands, and may include a slight shift with the hips and legs. Weight distribution ("pressure" for teachers who like to use semantics, but it is truly weight shift) in the feet can usually be sensed early—you are slightly off the left foot and beginning to move weight or pressure onto the right. The left-foot/right-knee action is critical to a proper one-piece take-away. Sensation in the feet should be slight, while the movement of the club should have an unforced, involuntary quality to it. *Hogan described the first move away as one of the two "crossroads" in the golf swing, but it is still often underestimated.*

As the club first moves back, your head may move laterally or rotate away from the target on any full power swing. Although the head naturally moves, *both eyes* remain on the ball. The head's slight motion or turn accommodates a rotation of your upper spine and weight shift onto your right leg. *Many great ball strikers have early lateral head motion.* It is not a requirement to move laterally, but many great ball strikers shift noticeably as upper center first begins to coil away from the target. I would also note that those who turn the chin away from the target are mostly left-eye dominant. Those who shift more laterally are almost always right-eye dominant.

Early on, the *axis* of the swing has shifted to the inside of your right leg. *Thus, the right leg becomes the backswing pivot point. The right leg is the post you will turn on. Think of your take-away as a miniature movement to the side far more than as a rotation around the center of your body.* Golfers who think "turn" as they go to Step One are highly prone to employing a "reverse pivot," that is, loading weight onto the left foot instead of the right foot. This would be acceptable for short shots and short irons, but is not recommended for full shots. At Step One we establish the back leg as the pivot leg or balance point of the backswing. You have the choice of coiling on either leg, but it cannot be both. So get into the back leg early.

Now let's monitor the club. The clubshaft stays between the arms through the early stage of the golf swing. For top players, there is no conscious effort to guide the club. They are on automatic pilot. The clubface stays square to the arc of the swing, with usually no conscious rotation of the hands. Grip pressure in each hand stays constant (at a moderate lightness). Often, in practice many golfers need to consciously guide the club with the hands and arms until they master the move.

Eventually the job of the hands is only to *maintain feel*. The arms, hands, and club are put into motion by the shoulders and arms, although it may very well feel like it is everything together. There is a sensation that the club is swinging away freely, with no rigidity of the hands and arms. At the same time, control is maintained: you can feel exactly where the clubface is located and how it is oriented. In a natural swing action, which follows an arc, the clubhead rises up gradually along that arc. Be cautious not to overdo the dragging action of the club or to pick up the club abruptly with your hands. Top players may use descriptive phrases like "sling the club back" and "pump it back with your left knee" to get across the idea that the hands and arms are, to this point, only along for the ride.

A proper weight shift in Step One moves your weight to the right foot and toward the right heel. It is important that you maintain some flex in your right knee during this step. The right leg is your brace. It accepts the weight transfer and helps create more torque potential in your coil.

If the upper body and hands and arms are used for the take-away, there will be no quick or jerky motions. You feel a connected motion. The pace is even and smooth, setting the stage for good tempo with every shot. Many times the only swing thought a great player will have is "smooth take-away."

If you have correctly established the right leg as the backswing support post, you will be off to a smooth start. It is a take-away you can practice and perfect. It is a take-away you can repeat under pressure and is the first key to consistency. Remember—it's not your job or your responsibility to pull the club inside the target line as a conscious act. This inside tracking will take care of itself, but if and only if your take-away is proper. Through the Step One position, the club may, in fact, appear and feel too far outside the arc of the swing for many players. Unless you push your left arm out and away, however, you'll never be outside; just stay connected, or together for Step One.

**Death Moves**

1. Freezing over the ball with no waggle and/or ignition before moving the club away from the ball

2. Leaving most of your weight on your left leg, to such a degree that the left leg becomes the pivot point
3. Overextending or disconnecting the left arm
4. Rolling your hands over dramatically in a clockwise direction
5. Moving your head toward the target

## Basic Guidelines

- Use some slight forward motion to initiate your take-away. A small forward press of the legs and/or waggle of the club should work well. Whichever trigger mechanism you choose, practice it and stick with it. Start your swing with momentum.
- Take the clubhead away from the ball smoothly in a one-piece motion (shoulders, arms, hands, and club start away together), making sure that your body stays level (does not dip or rise) and is free of any tension.
- When the clubhead is approximately three feet to the back of the ball, check to see if the clubshaft is still pointing between your arms, weight is moving just slightly to the right leg, and you have maintained the flex in the right knee.

## Mirror Work

Practice at home in front of a mirror. Take the club away by choking down to the steel—the grip end will be in your stomach. This will demonstrate dramatically the "connection" in your take-away. Swing the club back and forth to feel the connection between your body and your hands and arms.

**Negatives**

**1.** Raising your head or body

**2.** Dipping your head and body

**3.** A fast move away from the ball (usually with the hands)

**Spoke Drill**

As you know from reading my ideas on Step One, this part of the swing is a tremendously underrated area of the golf swing. I talk about this at every school opening. To illustrate, I (1) start from a bad setup, then (2) start the club away poorly. With these two things going wrong, you are history. Two Death Moves add up to no chance. Probably, the best drill to improve your take-away is the Spoke Drill: when you grip down on your club to the steel, the butt end of the grip will touch either your lower center or your belt buckle area, or be just an inch away from it. The club is then easily seen between your arms, and as the club starts away for the first two or three feet you maintain the original relationship. This is a basic one-piece take-away action, and the drill allows you to easily see that when it is done incorrectly the club will come out of center immediately. When it is done properly, as the club goes away, you keep the grip against your center during the initial move of the swing. Ingrain this move, and you will be off to a great start. You can also do this drill near a wall so you can see that the club will automatically work to the inside of the wall (or toward the golfer) during the take-away. It does not go straight back. The club will also start to elevate slightly; it does not drag on the ground. So the club works both in and up, and it also works behind and around the golfer.

Step Two: The classic "hand back" position

## STEP TWO: HALFWAY BACK

The halfway back position is the checkpoint where the clubshaft is parallel to the ground and the butt of the grip is pointed approximately at the target. This is an important checkpoint, although there is significant room for personal preference at this section. It's interesting to note that, at this split second, *the clubhead is as far from the target as it will ever get.* The clubface is square to the arc of the swing, with the toe of the "head" basically pointing upward. (Depending on the spine angle of the player during the setup, the clubface may appear slightly closed or downward—this is okay.)

At the Step Two position, when you're one-fourth of the way through the swing, nothing should be badly trailing or leading. The club, arms, and shoulders look synchronized and move as a unit. This is your backswing "package." At Step Two, whether you focus on the hands and arms or instead the big muscles (and upper center), things look in sync.

Specifically, at this point you should have (1) shifted some weight onto your right foot; (2) retained the flex in your right knee as you started with at address (there may be a little "float" and some straightening with the right knee, but not much); (3) retained the flex in your left knee, while it has broken inward and is pointing behind the ball; and (4) kept your right arm slightly above your left (in the manner of Lee Trevino, Sergio Garcia, or Tiger Woods) or well above your left (in the manner of Seve Ballesteros, Angel Cabrera, and Jack Nicklaus). You check this at the face on view, with the camera positioned at fifty inches or higher.

Step Two: Target line view. Clubshaft matches up with my left arm.

A note on camera angles: I'm absolutely fanatical on camera angles and camera positioning. All my teachers videotape exactly the same way—the same way I learned from Carl Welty. This means our research has been done the same way for forty years. When I look at your golf swing or that of any student, from a beginner to a top professional, I see it from the same angles. This means you get a diagnosis based on the same positioning I have used forever. Camera angles can fool a player or a teacher badly.

Assuming the video camera is at chest height, if the right arm is visible *under* the left arm, you have committed a Death Move, caused by either rolling your forearms and the club far too much to the inside of the ball-to-target line or leaving your body center still, in an all-arms take-away. In either case, you have swung your arms incorrectly away from your body.

It is important to note that the clubface position at Step Two is not tightly mandated. Nor are you required to have the clubshaft pointed directly at the target. Some of the top ball strikers in the world vary on these points noticeably. Sam Snead, Bruce Lietzke, Ray Floyd, Ai Miyazato, and John Daly, for example, take the clubshaft well inside at Step Two. In contrast, Fred Couples, Lee Trevino, Jim Furyk, David Toms, Andres Romero, Sergio Garcia, Ryan Moore, and Curtis Strange take the shaft outside at Step Two. All, however, are able to correct and get back on plane during the downswing, which is the essential key to ball-striking success. This is also true of many other great players. There is a rather wide corridor at Step Two, as seen in the picture on p. 89.

Slight deviations from the so-called perfect alignments and positions of the clubshaft and clubhead at Step Two are not to be tinkered with, if indeed you are able naturally and smoothly to self-correct them in the downswing. Our extensive studies at Doral indicate that about 30 percent of tour players go above the shaft plane and 30 percent under the plane. The location of the clubshaft and clubface in the backswing is sometimes very overrated by teachers. By mandating a so-called perfect backswing, sometimes all natural motion is lost. The exact positioning of the shaft at Step Two is definitely not a fundamental to great ball striking. However, there are limits.

## Common Errors and Possible Death Positions

1. No hip turn and/or no weight shift. This indicates that the legs were "dead" and the take-away was controlled too much with the arms.
2. Total locking of the right leg. Over-rotation of the hips or a reverse pivot accompanies this total loss of knee flex.
3. Rolling clubface open. The clubface has fanned and rolled too far open. This is caused by overactive, independent wrist and arm action, very common in high-handicap golfers.
4. Clubface in an extremely shut position. This error is the result of a manipulation of the club with your hands or an exceptionally steep shoulder turn. If you assume a weak left-hand grip or reverse pivot, you're likely to shut the clubface.
5. Excessive extension of the left arm. This error is most often caused by the player who pays too much attention to the adage "Keep your left arm straight." The long left arm is actually an overextension from the shoulder. It is indicative of an early disconnection in your backswing.
6. Right arm folding immediately into the body and near the right hip. The high-handicapper makes a conscious effort to hold his or her right elbow against the body on the take-away. This is totally unnatural, and it causes vital power to be lost with an excessively narrow backswing arc.

   *Note:* The right arm can fold as long as it moves up.

**Ken Venturi Drill**

This is a halfway back drill that I learned from Ken Venturi. I saw him use it with both great players and average golfers. It is a drill where you take the club to Position Two (halfway back) and hold. From the hold position, you turn your body around to the right, and then you lower the club to the ground. Next, Ken would put a golf ball in this second position and check to see if you created any poor angles. If you turn on plane and keep the clubshaft and clubhead connected, everything will line up at the halfway back position at Step Two, and perhaps most importantly you will have maintained the proper extension. Take your backswing, stop, turn, and take the club down. See if it was lined perfectly with the second golf ball, with no angles and virtually identical to your setup position.

## STEP THREE: THREE-QUARTER BACKSWING POSITION

Step Three is reached when the backswing is approximately three-quarters complete. It is an excellent position at which to stop and view your action on videotape. Here's what to look for:

- Your left arm should be nearly parallel to the ground and reasonably straight, but not stiff. It should also be close to parallel to the ball-target line to a maximum of forty-five degrees off the target line. If it is skewed on an angle that takes it way off the line, you're in serious trouble. This is a clear-cut disconnection of the swing. The right arm has pulled too far around. An example of wide variation of teaching this position would be Hank Haney, who teaches the left arm off the chest with rotation versus the "stack and tilt method"

Stacking the right side. Setting the wrists. Loaded at Step Three.

that teaches the left arm pulled much more into the body and at a forty-five-degree angle to the target line. Both methods can be successful, and my system recognizes this.

- Because the wrist cock is nearly complete, especially with your iron shots, the club and your left arm form an L. At this point in the swing *the club should feel light.* This is another place at which there is certainly room for personal preference. Some of the top players in the world cock their wrists quite early in the swing—such as Seve Ballesteros, Fuzzy Zoeller, and Nick Faldo. Others don't finish the wrist cock until later in the swings—for example, Greg Norman, Fred Couples, Davis Love, Sergio Garcia, Adam Scott, Tiger Woods, and Jack

Step Three: Three-quarter backswing left arm parallel to ground. Clubshaft and arm form a 90-degree angle.

Nicklaus. However, at Step Three, most top players have cocked their wrists and formed the L angle when hitting an iron shot.

> **You should have maintained the same "knuckle count" as you established at address. Your left wrist should not roll or twist, which would add knuckles. Nor should the club curl under, which would subtract knuckles. Either of these wrist actions can cause the clubface to close or open excessively off the plane of the swing. It's an idea I came up with to give students an easy check.**

- In a model swing, the left wrist is nearly flat, in line with your left forearm, and the face of the club should be pointed in line with your left wrist. We call this a "square clubface" position. Nice to have, but not critical. Again, there is no one *perfect* position at this stage of the swing.

- You should feel very balanced. *Note*: traveling from Step Three to the completion of the backswing is virtually a matter of momentum. A bit of wrist cock remains to be completed, but otherwise the impetus to return back to the ball is more or less dominant. From here we are set up just to carry on to the top, by completing the coil. We complete the arm swing and the full shoulder coil together.

- Grip pressure should be equal in both hands. On my scale of one to ten, grip pressure is five or less. Duplicating the pressure established during the setup is a good goal. Maintain what you had at address.

- You should feel that your weight has shifted toward the right heel and on top of the right foot—but never toward the toes.

- Your right knee should have retained flex and not be totally locked up. Right knee lockup tends to accompany weight onto the toes and also onto the outside of the right foot (a common but seldom noticed flaw). When golfers, particularly beginners, get stuck on this motion, they consign themselves to sloppiness in the leg action overall.

- Your chin should have rotated to the right and/or your head should have shifted slightly. If the head remains completely stationary or moves towards the target, the pivot usually becomes rigid and non-athletic. There is almost always a slight rotation or shift of the head to the right. Please understand—I am talking about the movement of the head in a full swing. The gaze of the eyes should not shift or wander; it remains casually focused on the golf ball.
- You have not over-rotated the clubface or your hands through Step Three.

## L Drill on Plane

Take your seven-iron or eight-iron and place a tee in the vent hole of the grip. Now from address, take the club to the three-quarters position, and *check for three things*:

1. Most important, is the knuckle count on your left hand the same as address? Do you have the same knuckle count you had at address (if you do, it means the clubface is square). If you see fewer knuckles, you have closed the clubface. If you add on knuckles (which is very common), you have opened or rolled the clubface.

2. Is the tee pointed at a zone between just outside the target line or slightly inside the target line? That is the corridor for that tee to be pointed. However, we do not want the tee pointed too far outside of the target line (where the shaft starts to get horizontal to the ground), and we also do not want to see the opposite, where the tee would point to a line parallel to your toe line. That would be too vertical.

Step Three: Two views of a 3 metalwood at Step Three. The right photo shows the safety zone (a combination of shaft plane and the Hogan plane).

3. Do the arm and the shaft create an L position (close to a ninety-degree angle)? We use this drill to check swing plane, the position of your top hand, and also the angle you set between your lead arm and the shaft of the golf club. It is a great drill to practice often, and you can hit golf balls from here. By putting the club in the correct position, stopping, and then swinging at a ball that is teed up, you might be stunned at how well you can hit the ball in a very short time. Give yourself ten or fifteen minutes and you will be hitting beautiful golf shots.

Another good drill is to swing the club into the correct three-quarter swing and hold for one to two seconds, then continue the swing. Hit shots.

## STEP FOUR: YOUR SHOULDER HAS TURNED 100 PERCENT (BACKSWING COMPLETED)

### The Backswing

Every top golfer arrives at the top of the backswing in a slightly different position. Also, there is no exact stop and start to Position Four. Starting down and forward with the golf club, this motion is proceeded by a move first from the lower body, or from the ground up. All great swings start from the ground. By that I mean there is a sequential move. There is no exact stop in the backswing.

This two-way action was taught to Venturi from both Nelson and Hogan, and then from Venturi to me. Step Four is marked by the completion of the back-around movement of the body and the club, just before the return move toward the target. At Step Four, the upper body has completed its windup and coiling action, and the uncoiling of the lower body is poised to lead the forward swing. Yet, because the lower body initiates the downswing before the upper body actually finishes turning back, there is no defined end to one phase and the beginning of the next phase.

Obviously, the flexibility, stature, and physique of individual golfers give different looks and lengths to the full backswing position. That is why I say to make your personal 100 percent turn on a full shot. For some, that translates to one hundred degrees of shoulder turn, for others, seventy-five degrees. Therefore, there is no one perfect at-the-top position. Having said that, certain basics for creating a sound backswing always apply.

Let me now summarize those universal elements and body positions, relative to Step Four. Just a reminder that of the 180 players on the PGA Tour, you have 180 different backswings. They are all at least slightly different.

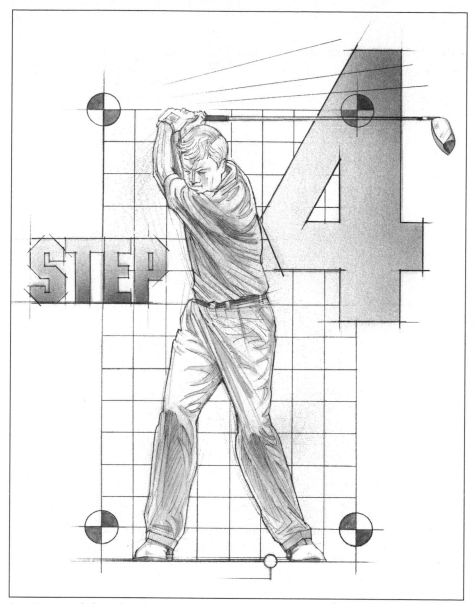

Step Four: Stack the right side. Loaded and poised for lower body to initiate forward move.

## Summary and Checkpoints

*Hip/Shoulder Turn Positions.* Throughout these step-by-step commentaries, the idea of connection is emphasized. All the same, at Step Four in the swing, the separation of the shoulders and hips is now complete. My original *Golf Magazine* cover piece in 1992 highlighted this key differential and the importance of a gap between your shoulder turn and hip turn. The left arm has slid up the chest so that the left arm matches the shoulder tilt or can rise all the way up to the Hogan Plane. At this juncture in a full power swing, your shoulders have rotated seventy-five to one hundred twenty degrees, and your hips have turned between forty and sixty-five degrees. This is a model for the wide corridors. Your left shoulder is behind the ball and close to being in line with the inside of your right leg. The shoulders have turned on an axis. They coil at a ninety-degree angle to your spine tilt. The shoulders are angled with the right shoulder up and behind the head. The left has turned under. Of course, partial shots like a punched eight-iron would follow a miniature version of this. For a general picture, the shoulders turn twice as much as the hips on most shots. A useful key is to think of the backswing as a major coil behind the ball. That image, which I wrote about extensively in *The X Factor*, seems to create the best image for most golfers, and it gets students away from a ball-bound weak windup.

*Knee Action.* On a full shot, your left knee is pointed slightly behind the ball. Your left heel may be slightly off the ground for longer shots. Most tour players keep the left heel down, but it is okay for the heel to come off the ground if it is "pulled" off as a result of a proper pivot. Under no condition should it be consciously lifted. Meanwhile, your right knee has retained some flex and is stable. You shouldn't lock your right knee, or you'll give up all the good body lines you established at address. Your knees have turned approximately twenty-five degrees. Place a clubshaft across your knees at the completion of the backswing to check. At the top of the backswing, the lower body

Left wrist and clubface line up. Clubface is between elbows and is in good shape.

has already just started back to the left. Interestingly, the knee turn is approximately 25 percent of the total shoulder turn and 50 percent of the hip turn.

*Weight Shift.* For a full shot, your weight should be toward the right heel and on top of the right foot. This is very important. If the weight goes well to the outside of your right foot or toward the toes, balance is impaired. RHP stands for right hip pocket back, a phrase used by Greg Norman. It's a great thought that works wonders for many golfers who make a faulty coil.

*Footwork.* Good footwork in the backswing is critical to good shot making. Therefore, you want to roll weight off the inside of your left foot. Ankle flexibility is needed for this rolling action, so practice it often. Also, connection of the left heel with the ground is important. On most shots, the left heel doesn't leave the ground. On longer shots, it should not lift independently. The heel lifts as the result of a full coil by some players. Lastly, your footwork should be rhythmic. Thinking of the golf swing as a dance step will help you accomplish that goal. That's a tip directly from the golfing legend Sam Snead. The great rhythm players all had and have excellent footwork.

*Head and Chin Positions.* Your chin will rotate its maximum distance to the right by Step Four. In some players, this may be as much as forty-five degrees. The average rotation is fifteen to twenty-five degrees. In addition, close scrutiny of hundreds of great players' swings on stop-action videotape shows that there may be a lateral shift of the head of between one and four inches, sometimes even more. This is especially true for right-eye dominant golfers. None of the great players freeze the head in the address position. There is always some head and chin movement. The head is not a stationary post, which is the Number One point of *The Golfing Machine.* Yet, remember that on short game shots and short irons, the head can and should remain very centered. On full swings and long iron shots, either the ball must be played forward or the head should move away from the target in a natural athletic motion. On driver swings, all the greats have some lateral and some rotational movement of the head. Don't let anyone tell you different! As Carl Welty taught me, "Don't tell me, show me!" All I can do in this book is tell you, and show you still pictures, but hopefully you have access to video and can easily observe this point.

*Left Arm Position.* Your left arm may be slightly bent at the elbow. The key point is that it be firm but not stiff, rigid, and full of tension. Golfers have read and heard so much about a straight left arm that they tend to stiffen it consciously in an effort to avoid any bend. In fact, our studies at Doral, testing every player competing in the PGA Tour event for eighteen years, indicates that approximately 95 percent of all tour players have left arm bend. It should be noted, however, that some all-time greats like Bobby Jones, Ben Hogan, and Ernie Els do have super-straight left arms.

*Left Arm Angle.* A critical observation is the angle of the left arm at Step Four. The ideal angle would closely match the angle of the shaft (whichever club is being hit). Fourteen different clubs . . . fourteen different left arm positions. The left arm would be most flat with the driver in this scientific example. The truth is that the left arm position at the top varies between the great ball strikers. Again we look at a safety zone. Some teachers want to match the left arm to the shoulder tilt. It was a big part of *The Golfing Machine* teaching, and something I have used myself. I feel this is okay, but very few tour players carry the left arm this low. Stay on or under the Hogan Plane.

*Hand Action.* Once you've completed your pivot, keep your arms and hands *quiet.* Many players, hoping to gain distance by increasing the size of their swing arc, will continue to swing their arms and hands upward after the pivot is complete. In fact, this attempt to pick up clubhead speed and add power to the swing usually backfires. Overswinging the hands causes disconnection between the swing center and the club. The clubshaft gets thrown above the plane and, on the downswing, will usually cross over the ball-to-target line. This impairs flush impact and sets up the slice or any variety of weak shots. *An excellent check is this: the point of your left hip, your shoulders, and your arms all arrive at Step Four together.* Remember to practice the feel of the hands, arms, and shoulders arriving at the top together. The wrists remain flexible, and therefore the clubhead will often travel farther back. *When the shoulders stop turning, the arms stop swinging.*

*Wrist Position.* There is no precisely perfect wrist position at the top of the swing, no position that will guarantee a return of the clubhead to the ball in a completely square angle. Hand size, grip configuration, strength, and the degree of lateral motion during the downswing all influence clubface angle. Among top players, Tom Watson, John Mahaffey, Lee Trevino, Tom Lehman, Zach Johnson, Fred Funk, Tom Weiskopf, and Bruce Lietzke exhibit closed clubface angles at the top, while Ben Hogan, Curtis Strange, José María Olazabal, and Johnny Miller, to name a few, have had the clubface open at the top. Parameters of preference are allowed in clubface orientation at the top. I'm concerned only when the parameters are exceeded and the student exhibits a super-shut or super-open clubface at Step Four or when the student cannot square the clubface from his or her present top-of-the-swing position. This said, I personally prefer square or slightly closed. Most amateurs have the face open.

*Shoulder/Arm Relationship.* The arms swing in front of your body center. Even though momentum will carry the arms somewhat up and across the chest, remember this McLean swing thought: **"When the shoulders stop winding, the arms stop swinging."**

1. Even if you had yourself in good positions through Steps One, Two, and Three, you are at risk of tipping your body weight back to your left side if you overturn your shoulders and arms at Step Four. That "little extra" you strive for at Step Four can lead to a legitimate Death Move. It is possible to overturn.

2. In a model natural swing, the clubface will always appear open in the backswing, then closed again past impact. Step Four should find it in a position that allows you to "get to impact square." If the clubface is turned drastically skyward (extremely closed) at this point in the swing, trouble awaits you. This position is almost impossible to recover from.

**3.** If you are wide open at the top, you'll tend to throw your hands at the ball through impact and hit a weak slice shot right of target. The wide-open position is very common in the high-handicap player. So use video to check your clubface at-the-top position.

*Right Elbow Plane.* In the time I have spent with Ben Doyle, Homer Kelley, Dave Collins, and other Golfing Machine teachers, the importance of the "back elbow" (the right elbow for a right-handed golfer), has been an important piece of my video analysis study.

The way we teach, in my system, is to view the golf swing from down the target line. Carl Welty and I have worked and researched from this exact view for over thirty years (Carl, for forty years).

The left shoulder moves down and around in the backswing. It does not turn level.

Taping in this fashion has many advantages, including on-course video. It is extremely easy to be consistent, a major key to quality research.

By plotting a line down the address shaft plane, we can easily chart the progress of the right elbow. The right elbow will track down the shaft plane from Step 5 to Step 6. I know that the most important line is the impact shaft plane, but for reviewing golf swings, it is still important to use the original shaft plane line.

## Picture Perfect

This image shows a perfect on-plane position at the top of the backswing. This golfer is hitting an iron shot, and the clubshaft is short of parallel. Notice that the left arm, clubshaft, and clubface all line up. The left wrist is in the ideal (or model) flat position and is in line with the left arm, and the

A great position at the top of the backswing.

clubface is parallel to the original shaft angle. This is a mechanically perfect position, as described clearly in *Search for the Perfect Swing* (Cochran and Stobbs). Even in their description of a model backswing position, they note clearly that there is no magical, perfect location. They talk about individual compromise. I like the idea that individual comfort and what is anatomically most efficient for individual golfers will be more effective and produce better shots.

I've been most successful teaching a good Step Four position by first teaching a solid Step Two position. With juniors this is a simple task. I have them simply practice a "hand back" move. With adults, however, it can take much more work at Step One and Step Two. Once we have the clubshaft, the left arm, and the left wrist "in line" at Step Two, it is a hundred times easier to achieve an in-line solid top of the backswing (Step Four) position. I find that the move from a technically correct Step Two to Step Four is almost automatic.

As pointed out in *Search for the Perfect Swing*, a combination of positions becomes much easier and more natural if the golfer can master the take-away (Step One). Carrying out the move from Step Two up to Step Four is much less complicated than writing about it or explaining it.

## Step Four Drills

*Split Grip Full Backswing*

From address, we split our hands several inches apart. As you go back, it will be very apparent to you if you make any rolls or twists of the golf club. As you swing the club back to the top, you will sense how the hands and the two arms work together to get the club back and pointed down the target line at the top of the backswing. As you do this you want to synchronize your body coil and arm swing. Again, with a split grip it is very easy to sense and feel. You will definitely feel if you close the clubface and twist the club down with your right palm under at the top. You will also easily feel if the left wrist crimps inward and puts the club in an extremely open position, a common Death Move error. This drill will give you the correct feel.

*Body Drill*

Point your left forefinger in the center of your chest, your elbow pointed at the target. From a good setup, coil behind the golf ball. This is a staple in our schools, and I call it the McLean coil drill because it is one of only a few that I've truly invented. I use this drill to have my students feel the upper center and to train them to feel and see how much the upper center moves. It also becomes very apparent how far the left elbow moves when you do this. Notice where you are at address and then where you are at the top of the backswing, and you can see how far back the center moved. This body drill is done mostly with the upper body. Put your right hand out in front of your chest at address. Hold the right forearm at a forty-five-degree angle as you set up for the drill Then get your right arm correctly placed at the top. You get a good right arm position mostly through body coil. At the top of the backswing, make sure your weight is balanced in the middle of your back foot. Keep some flexion in the back knee with your weight toward the back heel. Do not let your right knee lock, and you will be in pretty good shape. Make sure you get the upper center over the inside part of your back leg. *Also remain level;* do not lift up out of your posture, and do not drop down or dip as you practice this drill. To do this, turn the shoulders at a ninety-degree angle to your spine tilt. The left shoulder goes down, and the right shoulder goes up.

The most important move in golf . . . transition! The delivery position

## STEP FIVE: MOVE DOWN TO THE BALL

Step Five has two sections:

- Early (transition)
- Halfway down (delivery)

All of my teachers look at two stages of Step Five: first, "transition," how the club changes direction and falls into the slot, then, "delivery," halfway down. If there is a secret to employing a good golf swing, it occurs here.

## Early Step Five

In all the great swings I have studied, there is no evidence of a "stop" and "start" that together reverse the direction of the club from backswing to downswing. At this point it is interesting and important to watch the left shoulder. Venturi told me that the shoulder separates from the chin at this early stage of the downswing, and the left shoulder stays down. Many teachers say that the left shoulder should go up, but it does not in great ball strikers. Venturi knew this from his time with Nelson and Hogan. Actually, there is a slight drift forward of the upper body as it is pulled by the lower. The right shoulder is high and not pulled outward. That is, the shoulders appear closed as the hips open up. This creates a major stretch between the shoulders and hips. I call this the X-Factor Stretch. The arms, hands, and club also respond to the actions of the lower body or lower center of the body, which lead the parade. In fine golf swings, the last thing to change direction at the top is the clubhead. This, of course, makes perfect sense, because all the centrifugal and centripetal force we apply in the swing is designed to do nothing else but load the clubhead with energy and deliver it down the proper path.

## X-Factor Effect

I've detailed the sequence of motion starting the downswing in my X-Factor DVDs, in television shows on the Golf Channel, and in *The X-Factor Golf Swing* book. The illustration is a perfect example of how great ball strikers initiate the transition. The X-Factor is simply the gap (or differential) between

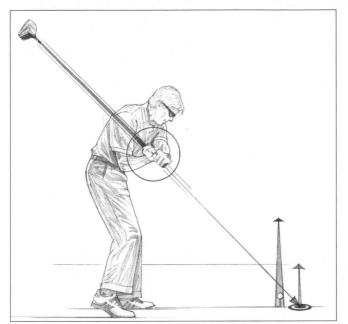

Shaft plane at early Step Five should point outside the target line.

your shoulder turn and your hip turn. A large gap creates torque and a very strong coil. It means that the shoulders do most of the coiling in the back-swing while the lower body resists.

*The X-Factor Stretch*

While the shoulders are going back, the lower body begins its shift forward. We call this stretching the X, or simply the X-Factor Stretch.

- The dot on the belt line represents the center of gravity, which is moving laterally and vertically upward.
- This two-way motion, with the arms, shoulders, and club still completing the backswing while the body center and legs are reversing forward, takes the slack out of your swing.

As the shoulders and arms are still going back, the lower body reverses direction. At this point in the swing, many players feel weight being pushed downward in their right leg. Others feel the left knee, right knee, or both knees start forward. To appreciate this unique technical point, notice how the body's lower center is moving forward. As the shoulders turn, and the lower body reverses direction, the X-factor differential, or gap, is increased.

- This is an athletically correct move that applies to a power throw in any sport or the hitting motion of a baseball batter.

*Right Forearm.* Starting down, when the golf swing is at a make-or-break stage, I check the right forearm (right-handed golfer). The right forearm points down the shaft plane prior to impact. During early Step Five, the

A great image for golfers casting the clubhead from the outside.

forearm should not be parallel to the ground at halfway down. This causes an open clubface, blocks, and flips.

*Right Elbow.* The right elbow returns on or near to the right side of the body in early Step Five. The clubshaft points to a line outside the ball–target line. The clubshaft is nearly between the back shoulder and the back elbow. The arms at this stage form a triangle.

The right elbow will continue near the right side of the body and near the right hip until just before impact, when the elbow is nearly lined up with the right hip.

An excellent delivery position: Clubface is toe up, and the shaft is on my parallel target line.

### Late Step Five

*The Delivery Position*

In the transition, your arms and hands are mostly passive and are still moving back as the lower center starts forward. The clubhead sinks lower as your hips start to unwind. Your hands and wrists respond to the reversal of direction. Your right elbow should drop into the "proper slot" by your right side and in front of the right hip. The Step Five checkpoint position in many ways resembles the Step Three position on the backswing. From a head-on view, it looks as if the hands and clubshaft are passing back through the same positions they were in at Step Three, *only considerably narrower.* There is sometimes a sense that the hands free-fall down to the delivery position.

If the first motion is initiated by your right shoulder and hands out toward the ball, and over the plane, you've got no chance to attain the correct positions at Step Five. Also, the down-tuck of the right shoulder can be overworked and cause a major problem. You don't want to cause your left shoulder to "overclimb" through impact, or the right shoulder to stall and drop.

*Note:* To clear up any possible misconception, I have not said that the first move in the downswing is made by the right shoulder. The downswing starts with the hips or lower body center (core) moving toward the target. The shoulder motion, good or bad, is a responsive motion that ties in with the hips or lower body.

Step Five: Delivery position

In a model swing, the hands and arms are passive during this step and respond to, rather than initiate, any action. The right elbow gives the appearance of attaching to the right side just above the right hip area. The left arm is extended from the body. It is here that good players feel pull, but that is only a sensation, not a result of any conscious pull with the hands or arms. With your right elbow near your right side and your left arm straight, it is easy to see that Step Five is a very powerful position. Your hands and arms have not "run off" or initiated the downswing but are simply responding accurately and appropriately to the body motions. The clubshaft is very close to the same position it was in at Step Three—exceptions include ninety degrees of angle or more with the left arm and clubshaft. Also, the downswing is inside (narrower than) the backswing. (This is one of my fundamentals; see page 13.) Your wrists are still in a fully cocked position. The club should not be outside your hands unless you intend to hit a cut. If it is outside the hands, this is usually a perfect illustra-

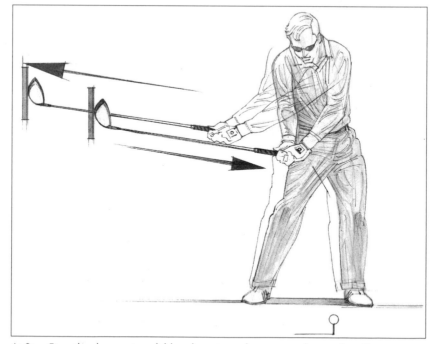

At Step Five, the downswing clubhead arc is much narrower than at Step Two.

Driver swing down the target line. Right heel just beginning to come off the ground. Good footwork on downswing.

tion of "casting" (starting the release motion too soon) or exaggerating the initial rotation of the shoulders. The "delivery position," as I coined it, will always show you the golfer's impact position. It is a critical spot in the swing that determines all ball flight. It is always a position I carefully analyze in my teaching.

## Seeing Is Believing

When viewing your swing at Step Five, in a mirror or on a high-quality video player, check to see that your clubface is neither severely closed or wide open. Having the clubface in the proper position at this point allows you to pour on the heat—to release everything in a natural manner without fear of hitting a nightmare hook.

At Step Five, body weight has shifted back noticeably to the left. It has at least re-centered the body and weight more fully left with short irons. The rotation of the hips is diagonally left, with the shoulders dramatically trailing.

Your belt buckle as viewed from the front has slid significantly toward the target, from Step Four to Step Five. This slide is a natural response to the feet, legs, and body that initiate the downswing. It happens *automatically* in a sequenced swing. If you monitor the belt buckle on any top player, you'll immediately see this powerful lateral movement.

At Step Five, the shaft should have traveled down along a path that, when viewed down the target line, is between the tip of your shoulder and your right elbow. If the shaft stays in this safety zone, with the butt end of the club pointing to an extension of the ball-to-target line, this indicates an on-plane swing and promising solid contact and good trajectory.

In viewing the swings of the amateurs I teach, I sometimes see the shaft improperly low—dropped beneath the elbow. In this case, the dotted line from the shaft butt hits the ground at a point well beyond the target line. From this position you will push or hook the ball—if you make solid contact. Often, you will hit behind the ball from this inside, shallow swing arc.

The safety zone is the area between the shaft plane at address and the Hogan Plane. I brought this idea out in 1989 (for Interactive Video V1), and many teachers use it in their instruction today, especially if they use computer technology. I now use JC Video. It is great for checking the downswing plane of the elbow, hands, shaft, and clubhead.


### Advanced

*Head Movement.* Starting down (early Step Five), the head is oriented differently for short irons versus driving. With the ball teed up for a driver and positioned forward (often off the left heel), the top ball strikers keep the head far behind the ball. Many have the head even farther back at impact versus their setup position. The head starts forward, or back to the setup position, and then reverses backward as the clubhead strikes the ball. The same player will have different head positioning with short irons. For many top ball strikers the head will actually move slightly ahead of the address position.

A far more common problem I witness is indicated when the shaft moves downward on a path that takes it above the tip of the shoulder. In this instance, a line drawn from the butt of the club would point to the player's feet. We call this "shaft tip over." From this position at Step Five, you will usually contact the ball with the toe of the clubface and hit a weak slice. If you manage to square the clubface, you'll pull the ball. Finally, this move is also one characteristic of the shank.

## The Sit-Down

All powerful throwing motions proceed in a sequence of weight shift, rotation, and arm swing, or "shift-rotate-throw." In all such acts, the quality of the sequence affects final impact speed tremendously. In the golf swing, "sitting down" at the start of the downswing re-centers weight just as the swing's most dramatic and important weight transfer is about to take place.

The sit-down is subtle, but feeling your left knee move back toward the target in a *half-circle motion*, feeling your right knee *kicking* at the golf ball, feeling a *push* off your right instep, or feeling your left hip start its *rotation* back toward the target will allow you to understand it better. The key move is a noticeable lowering of the body. Most golfers feel it more easily in the legs or knees. In the DVD I produced with Sam Snead, he called it a squat. However, I sometimes have success in teaching the chest to "compress." By that I mean the chest tilts slightly downward. It can also be felt as a split-second re-centering of the total body before the full power rotation into impact, and beyond. *At this position, a good checkpoint is to see if your thighs and knees are parallel to the target line.* From this position, the golfer will spring out of the ground coming into impact. The left hip will be higher, and in general the hips will rise several inches.

The sit-down can be encouraged and practiced, but it does not occur at a static, isolated moment, such that it can be attended to before the golfer moves on to striking the golf ball. It is simply a position you *move through* in the golf swing. It is also something you must practice to help your body understand the correct movements. One thing that "sit-down" implies is lower-

A typical high handicap move from the top: Weight is back, shaft is steep, clubface is open, and the shoulders are bunched.

ing. *I refer to this as compression.* Your body (usually the upper body) compresses downward. The head drops lower, and the golfer is in a very dynamic power position. The continued rotation of the hips, the firing of the right side, and the commitment forward to the finish position straighten up the braced left side of the body. The left leg will be straight or nearly straight at impact. From sit-down, we will move toward *stand-up.* The golfer literally pushes up from the hips. This is natural and will happen automatically with correct hip action, *since the hipline does rise for all top players from address to impact.*

The sit-down is a big key to hitting the ball powerfully. To master it, think *lower body resistance in the backswing* and then *lower body initiation to start the forward swing.* Practice a right-arm (side-arm) throwing motion, such as you would use to skip a flat rock across a pond or lake. Last, constantly examine your swing in a mirror. Make normal and slow-motion swings without a club to get your body actions into correct sequence. Make some incorrect motions on purpose, then compare the feel of them with the proper motion. You will most likely need to consult the services of a top teaching professional to get this absolutely right. If done correctly, this motion tremendously helps put the arms and club into our perfect "delivery position."

*Warning*: As the change of direction is initiated via the lower body, the hands, wrists, and arms are passive. A likely cause of missing the sit-down motion is that your hands, wrists, and arms become active, without your lower body moving. The result: The throw precedes the shift and the rotation. *When sequence is destroyed, loss of power, and off-center hits ensue.*

A related problem is the initiation of the downswing with the upper body rotation, the shoulders in particular. Results: Your hands are thrown much too far outward, the club does not fall in, and the downswing is too steep and too out-to-in. The golfer stands up too early and never makes the power move.

### Step Five: Final Checkpoints

1. The right knee has kicked forward (toward the ball or target line).
2. The hips have shifted forward, in response to your weight-shifting action, and reached the square position. The shoulders trail the hips.
3. The head has stabilized at, or near, its address position. The head often lowers in top ball strikers. I call this compression.
4. The right heel is grounded or, at most, slightly off the ground. At this point in the swing, it should never be extra high.
5. The flexed left knee is forward of your left hip. The left knee is more or less in a straight line with the middle of your left foot. The left leg is still flexed but is in the process of straightening.
6. The body has entered the classic sit-down position many players and teachers have long observed.
7. The clubshaft is on plane.
8. The shoulders are unwinding, yet still lag your hips in rotation. The golf swing depends heavily on connection, but in the downswing we also see two instances of *separation:* first, the lower body "leaves" the shoulders, then the hands and arms "separate" from the shoulders. The distance between your hands and your right shoulder increases as the club reaches our delivery position.
9. The right arm should be slightly visible under your left, starting down. Remember—the camera must be at chest height.
10. Your eyes are casually fixed on the ball.
11. The clubhead is parallel to the target line. If you stop the video clip at Step Five looking down the target line, the clubhead is attacking from inside the target line. If you draw a straight line down from the

clubhead, it will be behind the body and parallel, or nearly parallel, to the target line. This is what I also call the powerline.

12. Many golfers will benefit by *slowing down* the turn back to the target. Sometimes it is useful to slow the upper torso, other times the lower, and sometimes both. These ideas encourage an inside attack.

13. A big secret to good shot making is the clubshaft position at Step Five and the square orientation of the clubface. I call this the delivery position. I'm always looking to get the clubshaft on a neutral delivery path.

14. Supinate the left wrist on the downward move if your clubface was open at the top. This happens during Step Five. Sometimes we teach this move: making the left wrist flat or slightly bowed. If the wrists, hands, and clubhead truly respond to the lower body, this flattening should happen with no conscious thought. When it does not happen, we teach it. When you stop the club at Step Five, check your left wrist position. Look for a flat left wrist and a cocked right wrist.

## Death Moves

1. The clubshaft is "tipped over," or above your right shoulder, or the clubshaft is directly above your hands.

2. The clubshaft has dropped under your right elbow and is parallel to the ground (or almost parallel); your right palm faces the sky.

3. With driving, the body slides or drifts too far past the ball. This is caused by your weight sliding left too early. It is most visible in the upper body. When the legs go dead, the upper body will usually slide ahead.

4. The clubface is extremely open or closed.

## Stop-and-Go Drill

I'm a big believer in a full backswing, and the people who say the golf swing of the future will eliminate the backswing are smoking something strange. All top players will use a backswing, loading motion forever. It's wrapped into a precise measuring to the golf ball at setup combined with the rhythm and timing developed in the backswing motion. You lose all of this by eliminating the backswing altogether. The baseball analogy doesn't work simply because the batter has no idea where the ball is coming from and does not have the time to make a backswing that takes four-fifths of a second.

That said, I invented the stop-and-go drill in the 1980s to correct poor take-aways and bad positions at the top. It is an extremely useful drill and can help many students acquire a totally new feel. Even tour players use the drill, and in fact I first gave this drill to Hal Sutton way back in the 1980s to improve his clubface position at the top and slow his transition. It worked great after he almost whiffed the first ten balls. This drill also tremendously improved Peter Jacobsen as I helped him get back on the tour in 1992. He went on to make the U.S. Ryder Cup team in 1995. He won twice in 1993. It is also a favorite drill of Ryan Moore, who compiled the greatest amateur record in American golf since Bobby Jones. In 2004 he won every major amateur event including the NCAA, U.S. Public Links, the Western Amateur, and the U.S. Amateur, and he finished 13th in the Masters.

To do this drill correctly, swing up to the top of your backswing and pause for a few seconds. From here, just finish your swing, trying to hit the ball. At first it will be very difficult to make reasonable contact or any contact, but keep working at it. This drill is great for tempo, positions, and a better transition move. I see this drill used by many tour players at PGA events.

## Pump Drill

As you have read in my explanation to Step Five, this to me is the make-or-break move in golf; therefore, this drill could be the most important drill you practice. Pump the club to the delivery position in Step Five. Getting to a great delivery really separates the men from the boys, and good ball strikers from someone who is totally inconsistent. It is worth the effort to master this drill and practice it often. From the top of your backswing, pump the club down to the halfway position. When you do it, you must *make sure to do it correctly. This drill has to be executed really well.* You have to get the club lined up with the target or parallel to the target line. In addition, the clubface must be in a square position, the toe-up position. We can get away with its being somewhat closed in the backswing, but when we come down I want the clubface square or even slightly open. I also want the right elbow to return to the right side and just in front of the right hip, and I also want you to be into the sit-down position described earlier, where your weight is again evenly distributed or slightly forward.

Now, understand that this can be overdone. You have to be very careful that your spine is not leaning back too far. Your head will have returned very close to its address position, so if there was some shift of the head to the right on the backswing, there should be close to that amount of shift back, which is a very natural move. When you look in a mirror you can easily see what is happening. For a driver practice swing, you must not let your head shift ahead of its address position. If it shifts slightly behind that line, you are probably okay. So we go up to the top and pump the club down, and repeat, repeat, repeat. Do it often. This is a wonderful drill to do at home in front of a mirror. You can get a tremendous amount done at home, and you can also use this pump drill at the range. I have some students pump the club down to that halfway down position several times, then hit a golf ball. So the pump drill is from Step Four to Step Five from the top of the backswing to delivery.

Take the club up to the top, stop, pump, and then go back to Step Four, the top of the backswing. You go from Position Four to Position Five and then from Position Five wind it back up to Position Four, then back down to Position Five. Go from the top of the backswing to delivery over and over until you get that great sequence feel and the great feeling of the club lowering or dropping into that hitting slot. It is a super drill.

*The Left Elbow.* Starting down and just prior to impact, many fine ball strikers have a bend in the left elbow. Most teachers believe this to be a crucial mistake and would absolutely try to change it. They are mistaken. There are major championship winners, such as Retief Goosen and Lanny Wadkins, who have had this soft left elbow, which can be used as another lever to add power.

## STEP SIX: IMPACT

At last: the *moment of truth.* If you consistently arrive at the impact position with the proper alignments and sufficient clubhead speed, whatever your swing looked like in the backswing is *irrelevant.* Whatever small mistakes and swing flaws you committed along the way are forgiven. Just look at the widely varying swings on the PGA Tour to prove the point. To me, the impact zone is more important than just the moment of impact. In this small section of the swing, fundamentals include speed, center contact, and neutral swing path. It is interesting to me that most teachers say that tour players look the same at impact. In reality they do not. What is the same are the key fundamentals I have listed in this book.

Any player who can arrive at an excellent impact position consistently with speed has what we all strive so hard to achieve: a repeating (therefore *perfect*) swing—for that player. The look of a swing is, in the final analysis, overrated. Why else would we see so many champion golfers with highly individualized swing characteristics? The most important characteristic they share is this: they all arrive in the impact position with the same solid consistency. They all have a great swing path.

I have spent long hours minutely comparing the swings of top players and have come to this conclusion: All accomplished players, including such unconventional swingers as Lanny Wadkins, Calvin Peete, Bruce Lietzke, Lee Trevino, Annika Sorenstam, Phil Mickelson, Jim Furyk, Retief Goosen, Lorena Ochoa, Vijay Singh, and Sergio Garcia, stretch the parameters of preference to the outer limits. But would they have been better players following some "perfect" model? I think not. We probably would never have heard of them. That natural brilliance of a gifted athlete should not be removed if he or she consistently gets to Step Six. Ironically, at Step Six—impact—the key fundamentals in this book abound. For example, each clubface is square, each player's angle of attack is on plane, the ball contact is on the center of the clubface, the clubhead speeds are all high, and the swing arc is very neutral. And the left and right hands of these players are working as a tight unit, not fighting each other. By the way, a wonderful sensation to feel at impact is that of the right side "firing" fully and the clubface *covering the ball*. Jimmy Ballard has long used this phrase to express the feeling you get when contact is flush and the clubhead and ball seem to be united along the target line for an extra split second.

Ken Venturi taught me to imagine I was hitting "four golf balls all lined up" as a visual picture—an idea I often use in my teaching today. I learned many interesting ideas from Ballard, who was a very controversial teacher but was also very good with the advanced golfer because he taught ideas to get the club out in front of the body. When Tiger Woods and other top players complain about getting the club stuck, that means they have the club too far behind the body or they have too much lag. Ballard was great for this problem. He hated the concept of pull in the downswing; he wanted width. Nobody was teaching width in the downswing in the 1970s. Just pick up any book from that era or before. Now, thirty years later, many top teachers have caught on, and we read about it all the time. Ballard's idea for creating width has

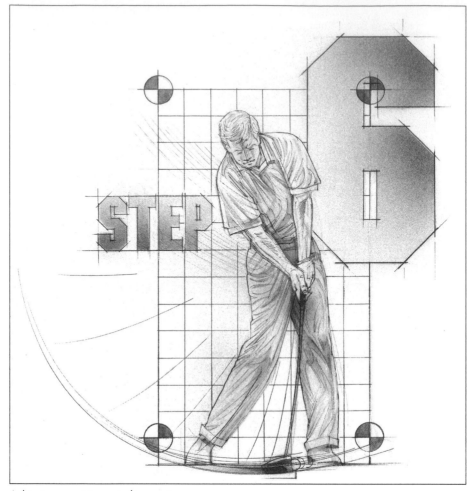

Achieving great impact alignments.

much to do with covering the golf ball with the toe of the club. I teach this idea to golfers with too much lag or who hang back and flip. The idea is to turn the toe down, or closed, early in the downswing. When you do this you almost automatically create width. Jimmy would also say "spring the shaft" or "kick the shaft" to stop the pull or lag and the resulting block or inside-out hook. If this is your problem, give this idea a try. I'm pretty sure you will be pleasantly surprised.

Here are some vital facts about impact:

Step Six: Down the target line

- The left wrist should go back to its setup position or slightly arched (or bowed, or supinated) at Step Six. The worst power loss you can experience is the inward collapsing of the left wrist at impact. Common causes of this power loss are a slowing down of the hands through impact, which happens when a player attempts to steer the clubhead into the back of the ball, or overacceleration of the clubhead, in which the right hand causes the clubhead to run out ahead of the hands before impact. In a still photograph, you can see that overacceleration causes the clubshaft to line up with the right arm rather than the left arm, as it should. Both conditions result in a great loss of power. They are not often discussed, but these two swing malfunctions are terribly common among high-handicap golfers.

- The right wrist must be angled at impact, not straight, to match up with the flat left wrist. The angle of the right wrist is one of the very few characteristics that might replay the look of the address position. Therefore, the right wrist must not hinge forward. The hands and wrists must work together throughout the swing, and they can't if the right wrist hinges independently.

- The left arm and clubshaft, when viewed from above, should closely line up with each other. The shaft cannot lag too far behind the left arm, nor can it pass the left arm before impact. Both of these conditions indicate serious mistiming of the swing.

- Weight has transferred to the left leg and is on the left foot. The right heel rolled forward as it is most often one to four inches off the ground with a driver swing; some players will feel a push off the right foot—an excellent key, by the way.

- The right knee has fired forward at Step Six, up to about your body centerline. An effective timing key is to think, "Right knee and hands back to the ball together." The left knee will still have a slight flex but is in the process of straightening up. The legs are spaced apart

Step Six: The photo on the left indicates the safety zone for shaft return. The photo on the right shows a front view of body alignment.

from each other, rather than having the right leg passing over and catching the left; if this happens, the probable cause is too narrow a stance, too much hip action, or overly fast foot and leg action.

- There is space between the legs.
- The right elbow is close to the right hip and still shows a slight bend.
- The right heel is not behind the right toe.
- (On metal wood shots, the head may be slightly behind where it started.) Your head may have dropped several inches, which most top ball strikers do as well.
- The hips and shoulders have maintained some spacing and a degree of separation. In other words, the hips are leading the shoulders. What the hips have done is clear well to the left as a result of proper rotation. The shoulders will also be slightly left at impact. Remember—it is far easier to slide the hips toward the target than it is to rotate them clear to the left—don't get sloppy and just "hipslide" forward.
- The hips rise up a little bit at impact. That's because we are using the ground as leverage to get power into the swing. Your hipline should be higher at impact than at address, and it continues to rise through Step Seven.
- The right elbow is slightly bent at impact, and the right arm fully straightens only after impact.

### "Toe-Deep" Divots with the Shaft Very Steep at Impact

During the downswing, many beginners have a tendency to employ the Death Move of swinging the right arm out and away from the body. In effect, the typical novice throws the clubhead at the ball. The shaft gets very vertical at impact, and the toe of the club contacts the ground. The result is a very thin toe-deep divot.

*Shaft Return.* **As the club gets longer, the impact plane is often higher than the address plane. The safety zone for a driver is between zero degrees (meaning the player returns the shaft exactly to the starting address plane) to ten degrees above the address plane. Most teachers focus their attention on the setup position of the shaft (address plane) when the most important plane is the "impact plane."**

Because impact occurs in an instant (0.0004 second), it may seem odd to devote great attention to it. Indeed, some students find it difficult to think about impact. Yet, I've found that working back from the perfect alignments of impact is an excellent teaching technique. Visualizing a perfect impact position and making lots of practice swings that stop at impact helps you feel the sensation of a good impact position.

## Head Movement Detailed

Before I move on to Step Seven, a note on head movement is called for here. Remember—the head will move differently for short irons and low shots. Often I see the head move down and forward of the original setup position. On the other hand, this same golfer will move the head rearward and slightly behind the original address position when hitting a teed-up driver. Unquestionably, the head moves during the golf swing. Trying to freeze your head in one location can be a poor idea. *Typically, the head moves forward because your legs don't.* When you succeed in locking your head into position throughout the swing, you generally create trouble for yourself in other areas. The head reacts very naturally to the forces built up as a result of the motion and turning of the body. To attempt to restrict it is completely counterproductive. So, allow your head its natural motion—with iron shots it is common to see the head lower and drift slightly ahead of its address position.

## The Pinch Drill

This is part of our chip, pinch, punch sequence that we teach everyone at our schools. The pinch is a small swing, where we squeeze or pinch the golf ball off the turf and then hold right after impact. You make a small swing back, and then—*boom*—you pinch the ball and hold the finish in a very short position. When you hold it, here's what we're looking for: *a flat left wrist* for the right-hander and the *club pointed back in center,* and also *the left arm (the lead arm) must be connected* (that means the upper left arm is attached to the upper left part of your body). I am just talking about the upper left arm—not from the elbow up, but about halfway up from your left arm to the top of your left side. I also insist that the clubhead is stable and below the hands. The hips

A huge part of my golf schools, mastering the pinch shot drill as shown in this illustration.

have generated the power, not the hands. Many people will go through impact and disconnect. Also, the club may be out of center; it is easy to be out of center by flipping the hands. The left wrist breaks down before impact; the right wrist straightens out. That is the worst possible mistake to make and the biggest power leak you could have. Or you might overdrag the club and have the grip end of the club pointing outside your body. Another very bad mistake is a sawing action going through the impact zone, where the left elbow breaks down and the club gets sucked in across the golf ball in a swiping swing action.

A lot of things can go wrong through impact, but the pinch drill allows you to easily see whether you did it correctly or not. There is no in-between here. When you do this pinch drill, you will be practicing great alignments. You will have to use good footwork, good weight shift, and good rotation, and achieve solid impact positioning, which you hold in the pinch. When you do it and squeeze the ball out there, you will be stunned at how far the golf ball goes and how solid it feels. It is a great drill! The pinch drill will teach you where you need to be at impact, what great impact feels like, and also what great impact looks like, just past the impact position.

## STEP SEVEN: EARLY FOLLOW-THROUGH

Step Seven has three sections:

- Past impact (extension)
- Halfway through
- Exit

I have all my teachers check the three stages of Step Seven. They are just past impact, halfway through, and then at the three-quarter position. For simplicity, I will describe the basic checkpoint position.

Step Seven of the golf swing is the segment between impact and the point at which your right arm is just beyond parallel to the ground. Some of the poor positioning and mistakes that occur at this point are the outgrowth of much earlier errors and problems, but other Step Seven mistakes crop up during and right after impact. The most notable problems at this stage tend to stem from a breakdown of the connection between the left shoulder and the left side of the chest. ***This is perhaps the most important connection point of the swing,*** and letting it break apart leads to two major flaws.

An interesting difference happens in this section of the swing. The hands-and-arms-dominant swinger will have more space between the body and the butt end of the club through impact. Looking down the target line, you will see the clubshaft parallel to the target line and also (usually) closer to the target line. The big-muscle-body-swinger will usually have the arms in tighter and closer to the body. Halfway through Step Seven, the butt end of

The half-swing punch drill. Our motto: Be Brilliant at the Basics. This is the toughest drill we use at our schools. Copy this picture when you practice.

the club is barely visible and closer to the body (farther from the target line but also parallel).

Here are two classic Death Moves:

1. The hands and the club overextend down the target line, the left arm disconnects from the left side, and the left wrist breaks down completely. When this happens, the left shoulder remains in view (to a face-on observer) long past the point at which it should no longer be visible. A hook, push, or flyer shot usually results.

2. The left elbow slides across the body in a sawing motion; in a face-on view, the left shoulder disappears from view prematurely, the left arm breaks down, and the left elbow points up toward the sky—the classic "chicken wing."

## Step Seven Check Points

*Step Seven.* Thanks to the symmetry that is inherent in a sound golf swing, certain aspects of a proper Step Seven will mirror the good things seen in Step Five. For example, a good player's elbows and forearms will be nearly level to one another at this juncture, just as they were at the equivalent point of the downswing. (Here you can lay a yardstick or a golf club across your forearms to test for levelness.)

*Late Step Seven.* Slightly further in the follow-through, an imaginary beam of light emanating from the butt end of the shaft will point directly at the ball-to-target line during the follow-through, just as it did at a corresponding phase of the downswing.

## The Powerline

Carl Welty and I made an extremely important discovery in 2001. We began to really home in on the fact that all the top ball strikers had a common denominator from Step Five to Step Seven. We must have seen this a million times for the past thirty-five years but failed to appreciate the groundbreaking importance. In 2004, I wrote the *Golf Digest* cover piece identifying the discovery. I called it "the powerline." Carl and I explained how the wrists released the club and how the top players had what we call a neutral swing path. The powerline means that the clubshaft and the hands form a straight line from Step Five to Step Seven. Looking directly down the target line, as all McLean instructors videotape, this observation might be the most important item I've ever discovered in teaching. I produced a very important DVD titled *The Powerline* in 2006, so if you are serious about this subject you might want to check out that DVD for an extensive visual presentation.

The power release used by all the golf greats.

One other important observation I've made at late Step Seven (looking down the target line) is that the shaft and the shoulder plane nearly line up.

Remember—looking up the target line at the golfer as he or she completes Step Seven, you should observe that the line of the clubshaft extends out from the line of the right arm with only a slight angle at the hands. The good player's clubshaft makes nearly an unbroken straight line with the right arm, just past this checkpoint position. Moreover, the continuing rotation of the hips and body center through impact allows the golfer to remain connected through Step Seven. This is another "top ball striker" fundamental.

This is also a point in the swing at which poor footwork and legwork can sometimes bog down. Keep your legs and feet driving off the earth and with your body weight moving to its eventual point of total transfer to the left post, or left pivotal point of the swing (your left leg). The right heel is well off

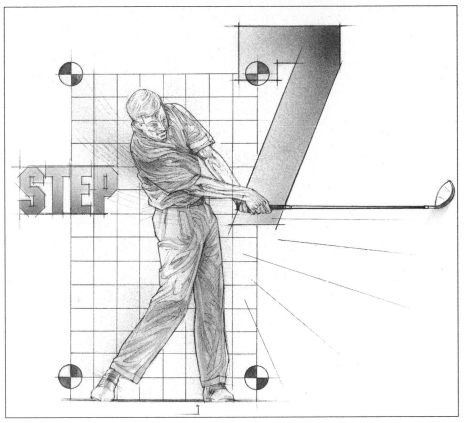

Step Seven: The power release and pulling up out of the earth with the hips

the ground. The hipline is rising, and the left hip is higher than the right. Going through Step Seven, the hipline should rise several inches, so practice this with rehearsed swings often.

## Take the Triangle Test

As a drill, practice retaining the important connections of your swing by checking the distance between the butt of the club and your navel. See that this gap does not decrease from impact through Step Seven. Another important check

Step Seven: Late target line view of Step Seven showing what I've termed "shaft exit"

involves the orientation of the club handle within the all-important triangle formed by your arms and your shoulder line. The club should remain in the center of the triangle through this phase of the swing. It should be like a spoke of a wheel, with the center of your abdomen acting as the hub. When the great Roberto de Vicenzo from Argentina told me he "hit the ball with his stomach," it allowed me to appreciate the idea of proper *connection* through impact.

## Negatives to Avoid

*Left shoulder climb.* Keep your shoulders turning on your spine tilt. In other words, avoid the classic "rock and block." Also, many amateurs will have the right shoulder too high and over the top—the opposite mistake.

Arms, upper center, and lower center rotate in unison through impact.

*Eyes glued too long to the spot.* Once the ball is struck, you have no reason to keep focusing on the divot or tee; in fact, you will contribute to a breakdown of your overall swing if you don't allow your head and eyes to follow the ball once it is away. Ideally, the club is moving at a high rate of speed through impact. Trying to stay down too long will eventually cause you to experience back problems. It is an absolute beginner idea. Instead, do not keep your head down. Many top ball strikers are not even looking at the ball in the impact zone. They have released the head (chin) and eyes toward the target.

*Legs gone dead as follow-through begins.* Impact does not mean that the legs have completed their task. Keep the weight moving and your footwork and legwork active. Keep your center, or your belt buckle area, moving. This rotation through impact is very important. Facing the ball too long will disconnect the arms and promote incorrect hand action.

Step Seven: Notice that you see no arms and no club in the photo on the right. The club shaft will exit in the boxed-in corridor, shown on the left.

### Drill Left Arm Only, Plus Body

In this seemingly simple drill, you use just your left arm, and you practice it both without the club and with the club.

First, we must learn to do it without the club, and as you know, I am a fanatic on doing these drills correctly. Pay close attention as you practice your left-arm-only drill. After you take the left arm back, you must start down with our correct sequence, which is a little shift. You might feel your left hand and your left knee working together, or your left hand and both knees working together, or your left hand and your right knee working together, but you will feel a little synchronization of your lower body action and the left arm working here. That is your little start-down key. As you come through impact,

> **The hips tilt and rise. Through impact the top ball strikers "come out of the ground." By that I mean the hips pull upward rather dramatically. The left hip will be higher than the right, but the hipline will rise several inches higher than it was at Step Five. Longer hitters might come up five or six inches. Amazingly, to most readers, the head and chest stay down during this dynamic action. I call this "compression."**

your left wrist must be in its flat impact position. This is the key to Step Seven. The release of the left wrist and forearm is done with a rotation of the lower forearm (called the radius). After impact we go into a hitchhiking position, which means that the left thumb is angled upward at the sky and the left arm is close to the body. There will be some break in the left elbow, but the left arm will stay connected to the left side and must not increase in length. You must not disconnect the left arm from the left upper quadrant of your body, and the invisible club we are using will be pointed at the target line. Now this drill is not left-arm-only; it is left arm and body together. There is coordination or synchronization, *a connection of the left arm and the body action when done correctly*. When you put the golf club in your hand, you absolutely have to use your body to hit the golf ball—at least to hit it with any kind of distance.

I have watched Johnny Miller (a phenomenal ball striker and U.S. Open champion) do this drill for many years, and he can hit a seven-iron 160 yards with his left arm only. I have seen a lot of other players do this. It takes a tremendous amount of work; yet, I would like you to eventually be able to just clip the ball off a tee and hit it fifteen to twenty yards. That would be great. If you can do that and do it consistently, you will have really learned how to use your left arm correctly.

Remember—you do not need a club. You should do this drill in front of a mirror to see how well you are doing. You must have good forearm rotation

Through impact the hips rise. A long hitter goes from a sitdown action to coming up "off the ground" for extra power.

going through the golf shot to have the upper arm work correctly and for it to stay connected and coordinated with body shift and body turn. This is a super simple move when it is done right.

## STEP EIGHT: FINISH AND REBOUND

In the final phase of the swing, your momentum takes you to a completed follow-through position. Your hips and shoulders are fully rotated, and the club is behind your head momentarily, before it returns to a relaxed, balanced position in front of your body. From this position, you just watch the ball travel to its landing area. The return of the club from behind your head is called a *rebound* or reflex action. This is the area that I call "hit and evaluate." When you hit, hold, and evaluate your shot, you are accomplishing three important things: **optimum *balance*, optimum *feedback*, and optimum *feel.***

Because all the motion of the swing is over, the finish and rebound are fairly easy aspects of your own swing to establish and evaluate. In a mirror, you should see, for example, that your right shoulder finished closer to your target than your left shoulder.

As you return the club to a waist-high position on the rebound, you should feel that your grip pressure there, as well as at the finish, is no weaker than it was at impact. You haven't lost anything off your grip pressure, in other words. Your basic grip/hand position from address is the same. This idea of maintaining constant grip pressure works very well as a playing thought. It is a simple concept that can help everyone from a beginner to a top tour professional.

If you are looking in a mirror that is pointed at you from the target area, you should notice that the clubshaft crosses through your head at the full-finish position. Its plane may well match the plane of your shoulders. I don't like to see the club flopped vertically over your shoulders like a heavy laundry bag.

During the downswing, weight travels across your feet in a rolling action. The front foot holds its basic position as a brace against the force of the body, arms, and club as you contact the ball. Turning of the left foot before impact

Step Eight: The pro finish

is usually a compensation for poor balance earlier in the swing and indicates a spinout. You'll notice it at your finish. Ironically, this unorthodox "foot fault" will help you regain balance as you move to the top of the finish, but the spinout is a bad sign if done before impact. Almost no top player makes this move. If anything, great players—Jack Nicklaus and Greg Norman, for example—may actually move the left heel forward toward the target on the downswing, to brace themselves further and to provide a force to "hit against."

I've had great success teaching "athletic moves." We teach moves that create power and can be repeated.

By making a balanced, athletic swing and holding your connections together, you can hit a big golf shot and finish at an exact stop without forcing it. Many great players practice by swinging full and holding their finishes like statues. Normally, the only time you will see a tour pro incapable of holding his or her finish is when he or she has made a hard swing from a dramatically uneven lie, such as on the wall of a bunker. But the poor player shows a fidgety, teetering finish on shots from flat ground. Avoid this, and be conscious of balance.

## Right Arm and Shaft Drill

This is one of our golf school's classic drills. We have the student swing a shaft with the right arm only (if you are a left-hander, do this drill with

An NFL quarterback is trained to get off the right heel. Throwing the long pass requires stepping into the front leg. It's the same basic foot action in golf.

## COMMON SWING MISCONCEPTIONS AND FALLACIES

1. There is one swing tip that will be your personal "secret," and you will never be able to overemphasize it.
2. You should play every shot off your left heel.
3. Place your weight out toward your toes at address.
4. Your arms should hang straight down from your shoulders when you set up.
5. All good players have good grips.
6. Barely grasp the club with your right hand.
7. Keep your head up at address.
8. Keep your head down throughout the motion.
9. Keep your left arm straight.
10. When your wrists are cocked at the halfway point of the backswing, the butt of the club should point at the ball.
11. A closed clubface at the top of the backswing automatically leads to hooking.
12. Pull the club down to the ball with your left arm.
13. Your head is the axis point of the swing, and it should stay still throughout the swing.
14. The right hand or right arm causes hooking.
15. Swing the club down the target line.
16. Finish high.

your left hand). What we do here is get a simple right-sided underhanded toss going, just as if you were throwing the shaft down the fairway. The club should whistle through the air and finish on the shoulder. Get it right, and you will have the flexibility or mobility in the wrists that you need to play golf. Most golfers are too tight in the wrist to get the whistle in the shaft. When they first do it, they may throw the club early. Instead, you want the whistle or your speed at the bottom or even just past the impact area. The whistle must not occur too early in your swing, as many high-handicap golfers tend to do.

Step Eight: Finish (top) and rebound (bottom), with safety zones

Right arm drill

This seemingly simple drill is not that easy. Like all the drills, it must be done correctly to be effective. Follow the instructions carefully, look at the picture, and practice it. You could actually do this with a fairly good-sized rope the length of a club. You could also do it with a wispy branch that has some flexibility to it. You could do it with a shaft, like we use at the school. A driver-length steel shaft works really well; it is a little bit longer, and it makes a loud whistle when you do it. When you finish the swish, make sure your eyes are at the target, make sure you can tap your back foot, and also make sure that the shaft hits your shoulder like Fred Couples, Davis Love, Tiger Woods, or Ernie Els, who all finish their swings this relaxed way. When you have the correct action, your hand will be about six to eight inches away from your shoulder at the finish. Your hand actually will not be resting on your shoulder, nor will it be too far away. The shaft finishes on your shoulder with the right wrist fully re-cocked.

The mirror is a wonderful coach.

*An Addition to the Right Arm and Shaft Drill*

We advance this drill by adding a step. Start with a reasonably narrow stance, placing the feet eight to twelve inches apart. Then, as you take the club away to about waist high (as the club is still going back), take a small step forward.

That gives you the two-way action a good player has. The club will respond to the step. When you do this right, the shaft will be going away from the target as you make a step forward and then swing. Step, swing, and finish. This drill, just an addition to the right arm and shaft drill, really gives you a tremendous feel of how the body leads the downswing. You might feel uncoordinated at first, but stay with it. Soon you will achieve the flow of the drill. Remember—the small step forward precedes the start of the downswing.

# 7

# THE TWO-STEP AND THE FOUR-STEP SWING

*Ways for Beginner and Intermediate to Simplify the Process*

## WHY EIGHT STEPS?

Many modern teachers use, perhaps with or without their knowledge, ideas

from Ben Doyle. Ben spent many years with Homer Kelley, who wrote *The*

*Golfing Machine,* and Ben taught directly from the book. Ben understood that

Homer's idea of breaking the swing into sections allowed students to under-

stand and perform proper movements faster. I want to credit Homer Kelley and his writings as one source for breaking the golf swing down into steps or sections.

I took numerous lessons from Ben Doyle in the 1970s when he taught in California, and he, like Carl Welty, and myself at Westchester Country Club, used a sequence camera. It produced eight sequential pictures of the swing that were ready to be looked at in one minute. (There was no video at that time.) I bought a sequence camera as soon as I began teaching in 1975, and I still have two originals as a reminder of my formative years as a teacher.

A dial on the side of the camera lets you time the swing to get different sections photographed. I got very good at timing the whole sequence and used it in every lesson (and I learned that every swing is slightly different). That timing device on the sequence camera was very sensitive, so you could move it to get any segment of the swing. If you did it right, you could get the backswing portions and the downswing portions in eight frames. Often I could get four back and four through. I would write my notes on the back of the photo and give it to my students. I also learned to look for certain positions and common errors. Eight stuck with me as a great number. It gives you an easy symmetry: four backswing positions and four downswing positions. That is how I came up with my eight-step checkpoint positions for video review, and the central title of my teaching system.

Remember—I do not teach all eight steps in a lesson. My instructors almost never teach all eight steps at any school, but as instructors we do use the eight steps to analyze the golf swing through the use of video. We will often show our students several steps that they need to work on, and how to check their improvement. I love that students have a way to measure their progress. I know that video tremendously accelerates the learning process. I know what to look for because of massive research using sports motion trainers, computer technology, and biomechanics. As we teach the basic positions to our students we will often divide the groups into different categories or levels of players.

## THE TWO-STEP SWING

For some beginning players, we may use two steps—halfway back, and the finish. We call that the two-step golf swing. By learning just two positions, the beginning golfer has two places they know they need to get. The positions are specific, easy to remember, and easy to practice. The halfway back position, by the way, has been taught for about five hundred years and is certainly not anything new. As mentioned earlier, if you make a serious mistake early in your backswing, it is likely you will never recover.

We teach this move by focusing on the golf club, hands, and arms. When the club, hands, and arms get into a good position going back, we can really help that person. We stop them and work with them until they set the proper extension with the clubface in a toe-up position. With the hands over the right foot, and with the left arm and the clubshaft fairly closely aligned, we are in good shape. I have taught this to juniors for thirty years. They learn it in about two minutes. Instead of Step Two, I call it "hand back."

As for the finish, I love to get players to understand good balance in the finish so that they can, *through repetition,* ingrain a solid finish position. At the finish of the golf swing I want them fully over the front leg, on the right toe, balanced on the front leg, standing tall, and with eyes looking level at the target, the hands and arms as in the picture on page 149. Also, they must learn to maintain the same grip pressure from the start to halfway back, and through to the finish. This may seem easy, but it takes a lot of practice swings for a beginner to learn. However it can easily be practiced in the home or the backyard. Learning to finish in this fashion has a very positive effect on the overall swing while requiring minimal conscious thought by the student. This practice will help any beginning golfer jump very quickly to the intermediate level.

## THE FOUR-STEP SWING

The intermediate golfer is usually ready for what I call the four-step swing, which can be learned in fifteen minutes. Once you know the steps, it will take some time and hard work to ingrain them. *You are going to come back to this book and reread this chapter, and I want to say up front that it is not easy to read something out of a book and then execute it, but with diligence it can be effectively done.*

So here we go—two moves back, two moves through. The first is the halfway back position from the two-step swing. The second is the full backswing position. Here you want to be loaded up on the inside part of your back leg and coiled behind the golf ball. Remember to stay in the framework you set at address. By this I mean staying level with your tilt and head position throughout the backswing.

The third move is impact, the swing's moment of truth. Impact happens in a microsecond. People ask, "Why would you teach something that happens in such a short time?" Well, because impact is so different from address. I think it is very important for people to understand where they want to be when they strike the golf ball. We do this very slowly, and we repeat it many times. We actually have many people start at address and then go to impact with no backswing at all. Get into a good address position and then shift the body to a good impact position, address to impact.

For now, to understand more clearly, I recommend that you review Step Six of the previous chapter. At impact you want approximately 75 percent to 90 percent of the weight on the front foot. The back foot has rolled forward, and there is some air underneath the back heel. The right knee is kicked forward. The left arm and the golf club are in line, the head is behind the golf ball, and the right shoulder is lower than the left shoulder. The hips—the center of your body—are turned toward the target between a range of ten degrees open to maybe eighty degrees open. I prefer the hips in the range of ten to forty degrees open. The shoulders are almost square to the target line and not too open. The hands are also together, with no change in grip pressure. What is different is that the left wrist, for the right-hander, has flattened, and the right wrist is cocked. The right wrist is bent backward more than it was at address.

This is very important and is quite different from what most people believe. To make the position of the left wrist clear, I often use a drill in which I have a student press the clubhead against a tree or against the end of the mat. Apply downward pressure on the clubhead. Of course, the concept is basically striking the ball with a downward blow. A check of the left wrist will show that is flat or tilted slightly at the target. It is a tremendously important position, so you cannot overdo the practice of going from the top of the backswing, slowly down through impact, and holding.

The next step is to take the club from impact all the way to the finish—Position Four in this four-step swing. We actually hold the impact position and then swing the club very slowly to the great finish position. It's the same finish from the more simple two-step swing—balanced, with the back heel completely off the ground, with only the toe touching, weight totally on the forward foot, eyes at the target. Position Eight in the Eight-Step Swing.

Those are what we call the basic positions: digestible pieces that make them a wonderful way to learn the golf swing. Knowing them will accelerate how quickly you improve as a player.


## Alternative Four-Step Swing

Another way we break the eight steps down at our golf schools is to produce many repetitions of Step Four to Step Five. We have the student make a solid backswing and hold it for one or two seconds. From here they pump the club to Step Five, the classic "delivery position." They hold this position for several seconds, and then we have them slowly rewind back to Step Four. Using the John Wooden formula of learning, first we explain how to do this. Next we demonstrate the move. Then we have the student imitate the move. Then we repeat, repetition after repetition.

Once the student has this down, we will have them go from Step Four to Step Five, hold . . . and then in slow motion move to Step Six. This sequence of Steps Four to Five to Six, when done correctly, makes for a dramatic new look to most golfers' swing pattern. After this is completed, we add Step Seven. So, the four steps can also be Steps Four, Five, Six, Seven. You can break down the eight steps in many different ways to improve the quality of your swing and greatly improve your ball striking. We do it every day with golfers at every level.

## THE EIGHT-STEP SWING BACKWARD

Finally, reversing the eight steps can be very productive. One of my favorite reverse moves is to have the student stop at Step Five and then reverse direction and go back to Step Four. We hold at Step Four, and then I have the student return to Step Five and hold again . . . then go back to Step Four in reverse. I repeat this action until the student really feels and appreciates the correct feel of the move.

## BEFORE THE SWING

Golfers make another series of moves that precede the eight steps. When I begin to work with an individual in a golf school or a private lesson, I watch for everything. By that I mean how they walk, what they first say, the type of clubs they have, the wear marks on the clubs, grip size, the clothes they wear, and then how they prepare to hit a golf ball.

## Golf Moves

I already know a tremendous amount about their coordination and golf ability before they make the first golf swing. I'm a huge believer in "golf moves," and the first key move is the preparation the golfer makes prior to taking the golf club away. In all my years of teaching, the most common reason students come to me is this: "I am looking to be a little more consistent." In order to achieve this, the golfer must be organized and properly prepared before every shot. The organization moves that happen before the shot are what I refer to as the "preparatory moves" of the golf swing. Before the moves begin, the player must gather the information necessary to hit the shot. They must determine the distance to the hole, read the lie, determine how the elements will affect the ball in flight (wind, rain, altitude, and temperature, to name a few). Once the player has selected the club and committed to the shot, the preparatory moves begin.

We start with the placement of the hands on the club. One of the major keys to placing your hands on the club is close attention to the relationship between the hands and the blade of the club. If the blade is misaligned from the beginning, it will be difficult to produce the desired shot.

Once the hands are placed on the club, I like to see the player have his feet close together and step forward with the right foot. For a right-handed player, this allows the eyes a wide spectrum of sight so they can easily align the clubface behind the ball. When placing the clubface, the player is able to determine their distance from the ball as well as the amount of necessary spine tilt. With their feet close in an open stance and the clubface aligned, it is time to place the feet. Depending on the club, type of trajectory, curve, and anticipated bounce and roll, the player has options as to how their feet are placed.

I term this beginning procedure "preparatory moves" because it is truly a matter of looking like you know what you are doing. To this end, I actually teach the moves involved in preparing for your shots. When you learn to look like you know what you are doing, you actually will know what you are doing. It's a rarely taught way to get better.

In my many years of working with Ken Venturi, I must have asked him a thousand questions about his two instructors, Byron Nelson and Ben Hogan. It's interesting to note that all three of those major championship winners also taught golf at private clubs, and to average golfers. Of course, I was most interested in the top ball striking ideas that Nelson and Hogan taught to Venturi. One thing that all three of these players did was a similar waggle. Another was the noticeable lateral shift away from the target early in the take-away. All of them had a definite "one-piece move." I played a hundred times with Venturi and watched him teach many others. He was an awesome ball striker, whom Nelson described as the best iron player he ever saw. Venturi taught players like John Cook, Tom Weiskopf, George Knudsen, and Tom Watson and worked with many other top tour players. Ken always focused a lot of attention on the "first move" away from the ball. Byron Nelson described it as "a rocking-chair motion," where the hips and club rocked together away from the target. It is very obvious when you watch Nelson's swing. Nelson, Hogan, and Venturi had the slightest drag on the take-away, too. By that I mean that the grip end of the club moved slightly before the clubhead. It is a "lag move" in the take-away. Many others have employed this same swing action, including 2007 U.S. Open champion Angel Cabrera.

The "rocking-chair move," or "drag take-away," is not fundamental to top ball striking, but it definitely disproves any method that says you must set the club early. I've seen no early wrist setters hit it better than the above greats, and I did not even include Nicklaus and Woods, two other late wrist setters.

I teach the "drag take-away" to golfers who have early throw in their golf swing. The idea is that the clubhead is the last thing to move in the backswing, and then the last thing to move in the downswing. Venturi also beautifully described it as a paint-brush stroke. If you were painting a wall, your hand would lead the paint brush. Another way to describe this is that you would "pull the brush along the wall, and never push it." It's great for golfers who cast the clubhead from the top. It can also be a great aid in stacking the right side in the backswing.

# 8

# THE GRIP

*Common-Sense Ideas and Tips*

As you could tell from my thoughts about the grip in Chapter 1, I'm not a fanatical stickler for precise hand positions or particular styles of grips. Some great players have grips so classic that their hands are immortalized in bronze—Harry Vardon and Arnold Palmer in particular. But several other major championship winners have had unconventional grips that bordered on ugly—Lee Trevino, Gene Sarazen, Camillo Villegas, and Paul Azinger in particular—and have been among the best ball strikers of all time. You see every type of grip on the PGA Tour; they are almost all different.

As I stated earlier, the grip—beyond being the golfer's only connection to the club—is not a true fundamental of golf. A study of the best players in history proves that there are a variety of effective ways to hold the golf club. The function of the grip is to consistently return the clubhead to square at impact while facilitating solid contact and power. A grip that provides those three things is a good one.

I'm always aware of a student's grip, but I deal with them on a case-by-case basis. If an accomplished player who is a good ball striker asks me to look at his or her grip, I'd be very hesitant to suggest anything dramatic even if the player felt there was a problem, and even then I'd be likely to offer only a slight modification to the hand position. But if a beginner or intermediate player takes a lesson and I can determine that his grip is seriously hindering his ability to hit good shots, I'll certainly urge a more drastic change.

There are some things I am pretty certain about regarding the grip, and the most important is grip pressure. Grip pressure is often more important than grip position, and its importance has been highly underrated. While some players play well with strong grips and others play well with weak ones, nobody has ever played great golf with a tight grip and frozen wrists.

I developed a "1 to 10" grip pressure meter scale for my golf schools in the 1980s because I realized that light, medium, and tight were almost useless terms. Light to one student was tight to another. How do you measure medium?

Generally, a tight grip kills your golf swing, and most amateurs grip too tightly. A company I've worked with (Sports Sense) proved that most amateurs increase their grip pressure by 25 percent or more during the first half of the backswing motion, while most pros barely change pressure until the downswing.

Yet, for certain shots we need tight grip pressure. A good player actually adjusts grip pressure from shot to shot—something that is not discussed enough. Even with supposedly perfect hand positioning, a mistake in grip pressure can prevent you from hitting the shot you set up to hit, or it can simply ruin good contact.

To check your grip pressure, hold a golf club in front of your face with the clubhead pointed to the sky. Adjust the feel in your fingers until you sense that the club is held absolutely as lightly as you can possibly hold it, so that it can almost fall down. Label this a "1" on the grip scale. Then slightly increase the pressure throughout both hands to "2." Work your way up to a mid–pressure point of "5," being as precise as you can. From here work up to the tightest pressure possible—a "10" on your scale. With practice, you will easily sense ten distinct pressure levels.

This exercise will heighten your awareness of pressure and grip feel. I usually have my students repeat this exercise several times with their eyes closed, which forces their senses and feel to be enhanced. Students really begin to understand small changes in grip pressure, often for the first time ever. Soon you will be able to sense different levels of pressure in each hand, which will greatly help you hook or slice shots. You will also sense grip pressure changes throughout the swing.

I advocate that most normal shots be played at under "5," with "4" a good number for the majority of golfers. For most chips and pitches around the green, I suggest a grip pressure of "6." With putting, most golfers do better at "2," "3," or "4." Bunker shots are best played around "2." For long shots out of deep rough, increase grip strength to "7" or "8" to keep the club from twisting.

Here are a few other guidelines for a good grip:

1. The pressure points in the grip should be in three locations. The first is the **back three fingers of the left hand.** Second is the connection between the **left thumb and the middle pocket area of the right hand.** Third is the **middle two fingers of the right hand.**

2. Avoid tight pressure in the right thumb or the right forefinger (this activates the tendons along the top of the right forearm, an area

The grip pressure scale I've used for over 20 years: Use the number system to monitor tension level throughout the swing.

where you do not want activation). The pressure in these areas will tighten in the hitting area, but that is involuntary. By that I mean that the grip firms up naturally through the impact zone. Yet, the player will do better to think "constant grip pressure" all the way through the swing.

3. Form Vs between the thumb and side of the index finger on both hands. It's a good idea to do this prior to putting the handle of the club into the fingers.

4. For a right-handed golfer, a short left thumb shortens your backswing. A long extended left thumb lengthens your backswing—just the opposite of what most golf books and golf instructors say. A long left thumb allows more left wrist hinge. Try it yourself.

When overlapping the little finger of the right hand, do what Ben Hogan advocated in his writing. Press the right pinkie finger down into the knuckle of the left forefinger. This helps unify the grip and helps keep your grip solid at the top. Have the distinct "feel" that you maintain constant grip pressure throughout the swing.

5. Hold the club up in front of your chest to check your grip. It is much easier to see exactly what your hand position looks like.

6. Unify your grip by closing your right hand over the left. When you do this, the center, or lifeline pocket of your right hand, should fit over your left thumb perfectly. This is a key connection point that should be maintained throughout the swing.

7. Grip more firmly with the last three fingers of the left hand. This activates the tendons under the left forearm. Do not grip hard with the left forefinger.

8. More pressure should be exerted by the middle two fingers of the right hand than by the right forefinger and right thumb. This is very important.

9. I look at the grip from the opposite side to see if the knuckles of the middle two fingers of the right hand line up with the forefinger of the left hand. Another fantastic idea I learned from Carl Welty.

10. I prefer to see an interlocking or overlapping (Vardon grip) hand position. They unify the hands, and as much as possible, I like the concept of "one giant hand." When you overlap, I like to see the pinkie of your lower hand fit in between the forefinger and middle finger of the hand on top of the handle. With this said, there have been fantastic players with various types of grips, including ten-finger and even crosshand.

# 9

# CLUB CONTROL

*The Two Distinct Ways to Move a Golf Club*

When practice-range spectators gather behind tour players and watch them hit one long, accurate drive after another, someone in the gallery will usually utter the question "How do they do that?" If they happen to be watching Camillo Villegas, Lorena Ochoa, Jeff Sluman, Sergio Garcia, Cristie Kerr, Anthony Kim, or some other player of lesser physical stature, they will probably ask, "Where does all that power come from?"

You can watch all day, but you will likely never really know where the golf swing's power, control, and leverage come from until you *feel it yourself.* A golf instructor's best moments occur when the students finally feel themselves swinging the club in a way that makes *full* use of their physical ability. Swinging a golf club is as dissimilar as it can be from such clear-cut athletic acts as doing a bench press. Unlike such starkly obvious functions, golf demands a complex series of movements to maximize the athlete's latent energy and apply it to the object to be moved.

In trying to take the invisible interconnections of the golf swing and make them visible to people, I sometimes use the following phrases: *the body hits the ball, the arms guide the club, and the hands fine-tune.*

Technically speaking, of course, the body cannot hit the ball, because the clubhead hits the ball, and the body is connected to the clubhead only via the arms and hands. While this fact may be obvious to a first-time spectator, the real workings of the golf swing are not. To me, there are two distinct ways in which the body becomes involved in the swing motion, and two swing camps. In one, the hands and arms dominate and the body responds. In the other, the hands, arms, and club respond to the body.

## BACKSWING MOTIONS AND FEEL

The concept of two swings is not new. In *The Golfing Machine,* Homer Kelley made the distinction between the swinger and the hitter. Most Golfing Machine instructors teach the big muscle swing, in which Homer Kelley recommended that the left arm be parallel to the shoulder angle in the backswing. Later, Mac O'Grady would have even more success teaching many tour players the idea of a no-hands release and big muscle action. Jim Hardy uses the left arm parallel to the shoulder plane as the characteristic of his "one-plane" swing, and the "stack and tilt" method essentially does the same, again teaching a specific left arm location. I don't believe in a manual for the golf swing where you "go to page so and so to see the exact left arm position" and so on.

Some PGA Tour players do keep the left arm parallel to the shoulder plane on the backswing, but 95 percent of them do not. I personally believe you can be a big-muscle golfer with your left arm in almost any position at the top of the backswing. Many big-muscle swingers have the left arm on a significantly higher plane than the shoulder plane. I believe it is a mistake to focus too much on the exact position of the left arm. Doing so seems to cause many amateur players to become too flat, so that on the downswing the right elbow gets too far behind the body—a very weak position. Allow me to explain my conception of the two teaching camps.

## Option 1: The Hands and Arms Dominate

This concept was made famous by the great Ernest Jones, who taught at an indoor studio in New York City. Jones was a phenomenal teacher and very successful with all levels of golfers. His teaching lesson book was always full, and he was perhaps the busiest teacher of his time. His book *Swing the Clubhead* is a true classic. Another truly great teacher, Manuel De La Torre, followed the Jones method almost exactly. I spent many hours with Manuel and learned excellent ideas for my teaching directly from him. Jim Flick, a more modern teacher, also almost exclusively taught the dominant use of the hands and arms. Players who employ this option start the club back with the hands and arms, and the large muscles of the upper body and the legs *follow* the club, or *give* with the swing. The body is thus responding—immediately—to the swinging action created by the arms. This type of action is best illustrated in the swings of first-rate female golfers or junior golfers. Their swings tend to be characterized by complete freedom of motion. Fred Couples and Meg Mallon are examples of professional golfers who exhibit this free-arm swing. At our schools we teach this "Option 1" to many students whose natural inclinations and abilities allow them to be more successful as hands-and-arms players. It is a great way to play, and my staff and I teach this concept to many of our students.

Fred Couples, the ultimate
free-arm swinger

## Option 2: The Hand, Arms, and Club Respond to the Body

This style is predominant in Ben Hogan's classic book *Five Lessons: The Modern Fundamentals of Golf,* which outlines brilliantly the basics of the big-muscle swing. Here the hands and arms move as a result of motion originating in the torso, trunk, and legs. To be specific, the large muscles through the shoulders, sometimes helped by a push off the inside of the left leg or left instep, initiate the backswing and put the arms and hands in motion.

As you can see, Option 2 is quite different from Option 1. In this second option, the body center dominates the swing. It serves as an inner engine to start the swing or perhaps to connect the arms and body to work as a unit up to the top of the backswing. Prime examples of contemporary players who

Watch and copy how the great players finish the swings. Often, this idea will help many other swing errors.

employ this method are Jack Nicklaus, Greg Norman, Tiger Woods, Justin Leonard, Nick Faldo, Gary Player, and Nick Price. In the past, Ben Hogan, Ken Venturi, Sam Snead, and Byron Nelson controlled their backswings with a body-center-dominated one-piece take-away motion.

## THE SEQUENCE OF LEARNING

In the hands-and-arms technique (what I credit to the Ernest Jones method), the golfer feels the hands dominating the movements. This is by far the best way to learn the golf swing as a beginner. I see much better teaching results with beginners and infrequent golfers when they learn this way. If he or she feels the body's involvement at all, it is perceived to play a supporting role. I believe it is correct for beginners and many intermediate golfers to "feel" the backswing in this manner. Try to let the body stay quiet while the arms lead the backstroke. The reason is simple: we train ourselves in steps and stages. We crawl, walk, run, and then finally race. Golfers should feel and learn through their hands first. You start by training your hands to move to specific locations or by copying the swing action of an accomplished player. You learn to control and square the clubface with your hands. Next, you train the arms to make a tension-free motion. There is a lot of "let go" in a true swing. Finally, you connect the hands, arms, and body motions into your swing center to become the best and most powerful player you can be.

Just remember that I might also teach much of this style to a top player, if it fits. To me the golf swing is always somewhat of a combination of these two swing camps anyway. It's not all or nothing.

## THE ARMS GUIDE THE CLUB; THE HANDS FINE-TUNE

The second opposite option for take-away and backswing calls on the body, or the swing center, to initiate or begin the backswing motion and create a free-swinging action of the arms. Ben Hogan said, "The body swings the arms like the pendulum of a clock." There is no thought or intent to guide the club into a position with the hands. The hands do virtually nothing. They go along for the ride. The feeling is that they are "slung away with the big muscles in the upper body and shoulders." In Jimmy Ballard's often-quoted words, "The dog is wagging the tail." I like to see the upper body and sometimes the left knee create a slight *lateral move* that puts the arms and club into motion. With grip pressure relatively light, the club is almost flung into the backswing in a totally connected, responsive action. It is the classic one-piece take-away motion.

This is the more desired feeling for numerous advanced players, even if they remain faintly conscious of the hands and arms keeping the club on its path. As you can see, we are training the hands for golf by consciously and gradually getting them to do less and less.

Beginners learn to control the swing with their hands and arms, whereas experts come to have less conscious feeling of hand manipulation for the standard bread-and-butter shots. Advanced players have trained their hands and arms through years and years of striking golf balls in every situation. The workings of the hands are second nature and happen automatically, although for specific specialty shots the advanced golfer will adjust grip pressure and hand action (fine-tuning). Ideally, the top player will feel the hands remain passive throughout the entire swing motion, although some players will definitely sense and feel the wrists hinge.

In a top player's transition move, the body "leans" forward while the arms stay back. This absence of hand manipulation is a high-level skill that takes years to attain. In my time working with Jackie Burke and especially Ken Venturi, they emphasized more of the big muscle swing. Ken had learned directly from Byron Nelson and Ben Hogan, and he knew that exact positioning of the left arm was not the answer to great ball striking. He knew and taught me that the teacher must use more body ideas at certain times, but then at other times focus on the hands or arms. It is often a blend. Jackie Burke taught me that golf is always a game of adjustments and upgrading. He told me that Hogan had "five hundred fundamentals."

Better athletes and better players seem to go for the big muscle of swing, from the scratch player to the tour player. Less athletically gifted golfers and those who play less golf seem to do better with more focus on the hands and arms. My contention remains the **building block approach,** using the gifts each student brings to the table. We don't get ahead of the students or teach ideas they are not prepared to incorporate. **First things first.**

Stay relaxed in backswing. Be careful not to overextend, which can disconnect the left arm and lead you away from more distance.

## A POWERFUL, ACCURATE BACKSWING: THE VIEW FROM FORTY-FIVE DEGREES

Those spectators on the practice range would discern the power connections in the swing a little better if they stood facing the tour player at an angle of about forty-five degrees off point-blank, toward the target. I particularly like this angle because there is a strong image of the upper body's full coil. I watched hundreds of thousands of Hogan, Snead, and Nicklaus swings from this angle. It is especially noticeable in the windup of the left shoulder. The left shoulder muscles (the lats and pecs) coil and appear to make a massive move back behind the golf ball. At the same time, the left leg appears to move—its movements appear to be synchronized with the movement of the left shoulder, but whether the leg initiates or responds is difficult to ascertain.

It is very clear that the actions of these two muscle groups are tightly co-ordinated. The forty-five-degree-angle view provides one of the best possible glimpses of the body's creation of energy to move the club on the backswing. The entire left side is seen winding the club up and behind the golfer. The clubshaft and clubhead, again, appear to be *slung* into the backswing. The relationship of the arms to the body has not changed from address, and we witness the *one-piece take-away*.

With the body creating the swinging action, this natural athletic move happens over and over; *it repeats easily*. Coming from the center and moving outward, the force can build and flow consistently. Therefore, the player builds a swing that can be trusted not to break down under the pressure of competition. Furthermore, with the body (rather than the hands and arms) initiating the motions, the golfer doesn't have to be concerned with specific perfect positions because the triangle formed at address is maintained through the first stage of the swing. Of course, mastering that feel for the swing is not easy. If it were, everyone would be a great ball striker. Mastering feel takes time and practice. Only after a period of dedicated and proper practice does it seem to become clear and simple. In the end, it is the most efficient pressure-proof swing, and it is truly easier to repeat.

## THE POSITION AT THE TOP

If there were a magic position at the top of the backswing that would guarantee all of us great golf shots, you can bet I would be swinging to that position and teaching all my students to swing to that position, and so would every other instructor! But there is no one perfect at-the-top position. Getting to a certain position at the top will work for some players, but it absolutely does not spell success for all golfers. An exact location or position of the hands or clubshaft at the completion of the backswing is *not* a fundamental. Instead, the key motion is in the transition and in putting the clubshaft and the clubface in the slot and on the correct downswing plane. You see in great golf swings *that there are two planes: the backswing plane and the downswing plane.* There is a plane shift in all great golf swings. The great news for you as a player is that a correct sequence starting down virtually eliminates conscious thinking. Whether you are in the "arms-and-hands camp" or the "big-muscle camp," the correct transition and getting on plane in the downswing are key to great ball striking. A correct transition will have the clubshaft fall into the slot automatically. You don't need to know all the details or all the reasons why it works.

### Why the Backswing is Overrated

The exact placement of the golf club in the backswing is obviously overrated, because every single backswing of tour players worldwide is different. I will teach you the most important things to work on for your backswing. We do it in the building block way. However, it will be *your* backswing, and there will be plenty of room to do it your way. The safety zones are much wider on the backswing.

Teachers often focus their attention on the backswing, I think, because it is slow and easy to see. The downswing is five times faster and is very hard to see accurately without the use of video.

## DOWNSWING MOTIONS AND FEEL

*To reverse the direction of the club from backswing to downswing, let's again compare the hands-and-arms-dominated motion with the body-dominated motion.*

But before going any further, we will continue the previous point by reminding you of this absolute: it is the position of the clubface as the club reaches the halfway-down stage that is critical. At this point in the swing, the

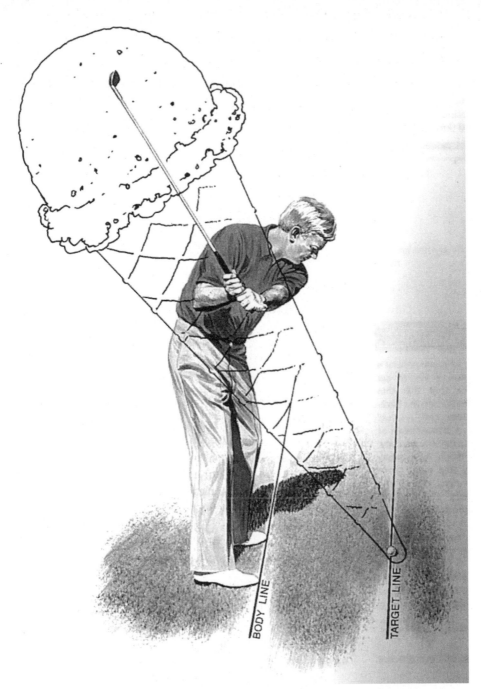

The McLean Ice Cream Cone: Combining shaft plane and the Hogan Plane for a safety zone

clubface cannot be extremely shut or be extremely open—in what I call a Death Position—where no recovery is possible.

In an efficient downswing that is dominated by the hands and arms, the arms initiate a free swing down toward the ball, with the body responding immediately. The feeling is of complete freedom and abandonment. The accomplished junior golfer is the classic example of this motion. Juniors usually have swings in which the loose, swooping action of the club pulls the body around to a full, upright follow-through. There is nothing wrong with this type of action, and I totally recommend it for a beginner and also for many other golfers who open up too quickly with the shoulders or who have too much pull in their swings. The hips react to the hands. Many baseball coaches teach a hitting motion in the same way, especially if the batter is opening the body prematurely. This is a swing that will promote "draw" shots. It is an excellent way for many golfers to sync up the body action with a better arm swing.

In a swing dominated by the body, opposite actions occur; yet, the results can be superior. For many advanced golfers, this is the best method under pressure. It's the idea that I work on with most advanced golfers and tour players. The force that reverses the swing's direction from back to forward comes first from the lower body or lower center (the body's core) and is relayed immediately through the upper body. The last thing to change direction is the clubhead. To do this, there may be a feeling of the core shifting laterally. The player may pump or kick off the right foot. There may be a feeling of the hips unwinding. Whatever the feel, the hands and arms are passive. They are put into motion by the weight transfer and rotation of the body. As a result, the arms, hands, and club lag behind, maintain width, and take almost a free ride into the delivery section of the swing. *Everything is loaded, and tremendous power is generated when this move is executed correctly.*

A correct sequence of body motion allows the right elbow to maintain the top of the backswing angle and also to move beautifully down plane. The club is definitely on an inside *attack track*, or slot, at the point we consider halfway from the top to impact. The wrists are fully cocked and loaded, ready to deliver a powerful blow. The weight shift forward and the corresponding right elbow move are tremendously valuable swing thoughts. These two movements happen in unison. Linking them together into a single motion connects the arms and body and delivers them into perfect hitting position. Harvey Penick taught this action wonderfully by having students learn and groove these synchronized vital movements of the downswing, often in *slow motion*. The idea of extra-slow practice movements is something all my instructors use with our students.

> Sense that the club "falls" freely downward during the change of direction. At this point the club should be square. To gain width, you may feel the clubhead close. Ballard called this "covering the ball with the chest and clubface."

## GOING TO AND THROUGH IMPACT

The only action required by the golfer from this perfect delivery position is to continue forward through the ball to a balanced finish, with 99 percent of the weight moving to the front foot. Centrifugal force, gravity, and an uninhibited free-swinging action square the clubhead. There is no conscious manipulation of the club with the hands as the turn of the body squares the clubface to the ball. This is the "no-hands" feeling top players describe. To repeat it is the concept Ken Venturi learned from Hogan and Nelson, and then shared with me in our lessons and rounds of golf together. If there is a conscious thought by the top players, it is to have solid or "quiet" hands and *an absence of hand manipulation through the ball.*

The clubhead speed generated by this process is always a pleasant surprise to the average golfer, who tends to see clubhead speed as a product of consciously increased hand-and-arms swinging speed. Actually it is the body that ignites the arms.

In another golf paradox, maximum clubhead velocity is a by-product of the feeling of *passive hands and arms, just the opposite of what amateurs tend to believe.* Part of trusting these physical facts is resisting the urge to throw or thrust the clubhead out at the ball through impact with your hands. As you'll soon realize through hard practice, you can get the clubhead out to the ball simply by rotating your body center. There is no need to throw the hands out at the ball, although this is an incredibly strong impulse.

## THE ARMS GUIDE THE CLUB

Because the arms are attached to the body at the shoulder joints, and the hands and wrists are the connection between the arms and the club, it is the arms that should direct the path of the club throughout the swing. If the arms do nothing but stay in front of the player's chest throughout the swing, and if he or she has correct ball position and correct body motions, the club must swing on an inside-to-inside arc. The shift action from the right foot to the left foot allows an elongated circle and a longer on-line motion—still, of course, inside-to-inside. The hips rise upward throughout the impact zone. Jimmy Ballard used to say "to hit down, you must be up." Jimmy used the visual picture and/or the feel of squeezing a dime between the buttocks (sorry if that comes across as vulgar, but in fact it accurately defines what happens). No question—you come "out of the ground," and the left hip in particular rises dramatically. At our golf schools, Dr. Rob Neal uses biomechanics to prove this point to our students. All top players rise. The hips do not stay level, and they do not stay down, once again proving that often the logical thought is exactly incorrect in the game of golf. Remember—golf is a two-sided game. Tension or conscious pulling of the front arm usually causes an open clubface at impact. It can be a real surprise killer. The feeling of "pull" is just that—only a feel. Once you consciously pull the left arm, you are likely dead in the water.

## SHOULDER ROTATION

To clarify further the role of the arms in directing the path of the club, it should be kept in mind that in a model swing the shoulders rotate at a ninety-degree angle to the spine angle. Since there is side bending in the swing and we play off different lie angles and with fourteen different clubs, and since all golfers have different physical features, I cannot tell you any exact setup angles. However, the concept of the shoulders turning on an axis is very simple and helpful. This is a very natural path for the shoulders to follow and introduces no artificial angles or club manipulation during the backswing or forward swing. The shoulders turn on an axis, and there must be a smooth and constant rotation through to the finish—something that cannot be taken for granted. This helps put the clubshaft on a completely natural—and therefore repeatable—plane. The arms, then, respond to the motions of the body and move with the body. This keeps the arms in front of the body.

It is important to note that the right shoulder stays up for a split second as the forward shift begins. Once you are on the left post, the shoulder will lower dramatically and go under the chin. The better player needs to avoid conscious efforts to lower the right shoulder too much by sliding the lower body laterally, because this action creates a swing plane that's too deep from the inside. The advanced player should feel the right shoulder staying high and the left shoulder down while starting forward.

Clubface control by the hands becomes far easier under the passive-arms, passive-hands approach. However, it does demand proper use of the body. By keeping the hands unified with constant grip pressure, you relegate the left hand and left wrist to a single responsibility—to *not break down! Inward*

The backswing shoulder coil.

The right shoulder moves down and out.

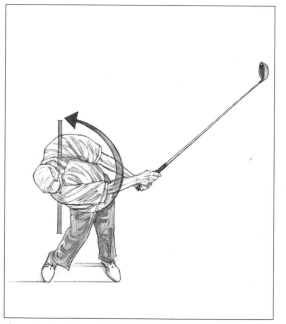

The right shoulder and left shoulder continue to rotate.

Rotate all the way through to a Pro Finish with the shoulders turned well left of the target.

*bending of the left wrist before impact is probably the biggest power leak in the swing. It is a Death Move for power!* When the hands are in sync, there is no requirement for independent wrist action or for any conscious use of the hands to manipulate the clubface to produce your normal repeating ball flight.

It's my observation that the greatest players in history have particularly emphasized "no hands" when speaking about their swings: Jack Nicklaus, Nick Price, Ben Hogan, Tiger Woods, Vijay Singh. Does this mean they have had no hand action? Of course it doesn't. To be great players, they have had to have their hands working and releasing perfectly. What it does mean is that they were not manipulating with their hands. They did not have to consciously think about hand action. Their hands and wrists were trained and had no responsibility in the swing other than to hold on and go along for the ride. The feeling might be that the hands maintain the address position throughout the swing. With great golfers, the hands respond automatically to the exquisite body motion.

The shift action creates an inside-to-inside elongated "flat" spot in the swing.

## THE HANDS FINE-TUNE

When it comes to specialty shots and purposely curved shots, of course, conscious hand action and variations in grip pressure do come into play. To hit a low slice or a high hook, the player will use the hands differently than when he or she hits a standard shot. Partially through setup, partially through visualization, and partially through a conscious swing thought that includes wrist/hand action, the player will adjust to the special situation. The hands come into these special predicaments and *fine-tune* the swing action to produce various curving shots.

## WHERE TIMING COMES IN

Under pressure of competition, a swing whose tempo and timing are controlled mostly by the big muscles will be more reliable. Logic alone will tell you that trying to time the hands when the heat is on is a tough task. When it's time to fine-tune the swing to produce hooks, slices, high shots, and low shots, the hands are there to hold the club differently, to vary the grip pressure, to hold on through impact (block release), or otherwise to play a part. From Step Five on in my Eight-Step Swing System, in the big muscle swing it's as if the hands do nothing. In the hands-and-arms-dominated swing, there is a free release and a feeling that the club pulls the player up to the finish. A strong body turn is what enables the golfer to hammer the ball.

No matter how you swing the golf club, timing and tempo are always crucial. Even the greatest ball strikers are constantly adjusting and finding their timing on a daily basis. Golf is, in fact, a game of adjustments. It's a game of upgrading, and that's what this book can do for you. It shows you many ways to adjust and also helps you understand what is not important. I've explained the two basic swing camps—the release and non-release concepts—but

Swinging with your right hand only will improve your swing and driving skills.

both still rely on timing up the body, the arms, and the club. Realize that some days you might need more focus on your arms and less on rotation. Next week it might be just the opposite. The goal is to sync up the motion and to make it as fluid and simple as possible. At times, when a top player is hitting on all cylinders, the golf swing looks and feels super simple. That only happens through hard work, talent, and good fundamentals combined with great timing. So think of golf being simple but, as Einstein said, not too simple.

A good teacher needs to be focused on the lesson.

# 10

# DRIVING GREATNESS

*The Art of Driving the Ball with Authority*

*"If you can't drive the ball, you can't play good golf."*

—BEN HOGAN

*"The most important club in the bag, in my opinion, is the driver."*

—BYRON NELSON

These statements by two of golf's greatest players cannot be ignored.

Although a strong argument can be made that good putting is the most

efficient way to lower scores, a reliable driving game seems to be a common denominator of all golf champions. You cannot underestimate the importance of driving the ball well. A successful drive off the first tee sets a positive tone for the entire round, no matter what level player you are. *Jack Nicklaus has even called it the most important shot of the day.* If you can consistently hit the ball far down the fairway, you are a skilled driver with a tremendous competitive advantage. Good driving puts you in an offensive position, whereas weak driving puts you in a defensive position. Long and straight driving gave Tiger Woods his biggest advantage when he burst upon the scene, and his loss of accuracy off the tee was the key reason he temporarily lost his position as Number One in the world for awhile. When his driving improved, he became close to unbeatable once again. Even the great Seve Ballesteros, in his heyday an incredible driver of the golf ball, stopped winning when he lost the ability to find the fairway with any regularity.

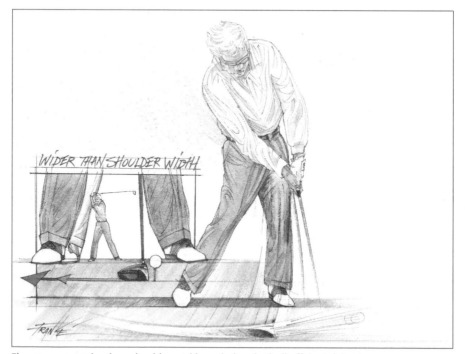

The stance is wider than shoulder width and play the ball off the left heel.

This chapter is devoted to the unique requirements and tactics of driving. I would like to share some important *setup* adjustments and *mental* adjustments that are unique to the driver swing and can greatly aid your performance off the tee. Ken Venturi's influence is evident throughout my statements and writings about the golf swing, and his approach to driving impresses me as much today as it did in the mid-1970s. During that period, I played many rounds with Venturi, witnessing a master shot-maker at work. I've been around some tremendous ball strikers. I roomed with Bruce Lietzke, Bill Rogers, and

Two driving tips emphasized by Ken Venturi were to assume a wide base and to lower your center of gravity.

John Mahaffey at the University of Houston, and I have played numerous competitive rounds with Lanny Wadkins, Tom Kite, Ben Crenshaw, Johnny Miller, and others, but none of them could maneuver the ball with better precision than Venturi. When I played with him—away from tournament pressure, when putting did not matter—Venturi could still do absolutely anything with the golf ball, on command. Here are the best driving tips he has shared with me.

**Use a wide base.** The best drivers place their feet wider than shoulder width apart. Past professionals who were considered premier drivers and who played from a wide base include Ben Hogan and Byron Nelson. Today, Jack Nicklaus, Greg Norman, Tiger Woods, Lee Trevino, Arnold Palmer, and Bruce Lietzke depend on the same setup key. The wide base encourages a shallower swing and an elongated "flat spot" through the hitting area, which is ideal for accurate driving. The wide stance provides a low center of gravity for stability and allows a player to "pump" the feet off the ground more powerfully. If you had one chance to deliver your hardest punch and win the heavyweight crown, you would instinctively spread your feet. When a baseball slugger connects with power, it's because he or she has stepped forward and hit from a broad base.

**Play the ball off your left heel.** This ball position takes maximum advantage of the flat spot in your sweeping driver swing.

**Favor a fade.** Many top-end advanced golfers play a fade because they find it to be the ideal control shot in golf. If you're strong and have good hand–eye coordination, try it. It is a great way to eliminate the left side of every fairway.

Bruce Lietzke has also been one of the finest drivers in the game's history, and he's retained that skill since joining the Champions Tour (as evidenced by his victory at the 2003 U.S. Senior Open). I played a ton of golf with Bruce during our days at Houston. We often roomed together on the mini-tours, and in his regular tour career he often stayed at our home in Florida during the Honda Classic. We've spent a lot of time talking about the game, and he was brilliant about figuring out what worked best for him, especially when it came to driving the golf ball.

Lietzke has reduced all his planning and thinking to a bare minimum. Every drive he hits is the same: He aims down the left side of every fairway, visualizing the ball *fading* into the center of the landing area. He addresses his ball and trusts his swing. Then he lets go with a wonderfully free release of the club . . . he lets go. Lietzke's power fade perennially placed him at or near the top of the PGA Tour's total driving statistic, which combines distance and accuracy.

An average putter at best, Lietzke rarely practices and has long played a limited schedule. Supertalented? Yes, but Lietzke also has superior golf smarts. He eliminates the left side of every hole on every golf course he plays. The certainty that he can only miss one way allows Lietzke to stay on the offensive at all times, especially down the stretch. If you look up his final-round scoring average over his career, you'll see it is one of the best ever. One major reason for his Sunday success is his ability to drive it long and straight all the way to the last hole.

Lee Trevino's practice sessions are a vital part of his preround battle plan.

**HOW TO FIGHT FIRST-TEE FRIGHT**

1. On the driving range before the round, imagine the shot you'll need on the first tee, then aim at a particular area to simulate the first fairway.

2. Select the long club that you play with the most confidence. For many golfers, the three-wood is the best selection.

3. Approach the ball from behind, focusing hard on your landing area and visualizing a perfect drive hitting it.

4. At address, depend on one swing thought that you know works. Do not freeze over the ball, running through a long checklist of swing keys in your head.

5. Once you feel comfortable, make an uninhibited, tension-free swing. Let go!

The varying techniques of Ben Hogan (left), Jack Nicklaus (center), and John Daly (right) show that there is no one perfect way to swing.

I hold up Lietzke's driving game as a model for my students to emulate. Especially in your driving, go up there with a plan, a visual picture, and a chosen shot shape. Eliminate every variable you can. Keep your plan and all your thoughts as simple as possible.

Of course, you may naturally ask, "What does Bruce Lietzke do when he comes to a hole that requires a right-to-left tee shot?" The answer is simple: he hits his three-wood. As Bruce says, "My driver is not allowed to know it can hook the ball."

Along with Lietzke, there have been quite a few other top performers whose driving games have been based on a controlled, powerful fade. Jack Nicklaus, Ben Hogan, Lee Trevino, Tiger Woods, Sergio Garcia, Vijay Singh, and Hale Irwin all played the power fade. For aspiring players, this should be food for thought.

## A LITTLE HELP FROM MY FRIENDS

### A Driving Tip from Al Mengert

The first golf lessons I ever took, in Seattle in 1966, were from Al Mengert, who had worked under Claude Harmon at Winged Foot and Tommy Armour in Boca Raton. Mengert showed me that from the tee, the fairway is actually a *three-lane highway*.

If you play a draw, you should aim down the right lane and plan to land the ball on the center lane (middle of fairway). If you happen to hit a straight ball that doesn't draw, you end up in the right lane—the right side of the fairway, which is fine. If you hit your planned shot, you are dead center: "Position A." If you hit too much hook, chances are you will still end up in the left lane of the fairway. Here's a good driving rule: never aim a drive so that a straight ball will go into trouble. This "driver's education lesson" will allow you to use the *whole fairway* and increase your chances of staying on the short grass.

### A Driving Tip from Jackie Burke

When I played on the golf team at the University of Houston, we had the opportunity to play with and learn from Jackie Burke, one of golf's finest thinkers, who won both the Masters and the PGA championships. Burke didn't just suggest to us that we "let go with the driver," he preached it nonstop! He found the idea of guiding or steering your drives totally repugnant. "Let go. Give up control. Abandonment." Those were the ideas he adhered to in regard to driving. To be great, he told us, "you must have some *recklessness* to your swing."

One of the funniest but most valuable times I have ever had with Jackie was when I was attending Houston and visited him at Champions. After complaining about my tee shots, he suggested I drive down to Galveston, Texas, and hit a few drivers into the Gulf of Mexico. A few weeks later, when I saw him again, he asked me, "What did you learn?" My answer was "I'm not sure." Burke then asked me, "Well, how did you hit them?" I told him, "I hit them great." Jackie then said with great passion, "That's it, you dumb SOB; that's the answer. Hit every drive like you are hitting into the Gulf of Mexico—or better yet for you, McLean, think of hitting into the Atlantic Ocean."

That single thought—"Imagine you are hitting your drive into the Atlantic Ocean"—helped me get through some tremendously stressful tournament situations in decent fashion. If you use visualization well, you will rid your mind of interference and fear. You will feel there is no way to miss, so you swing freely and with amazing frequency actually hit the ball on a string. I highly recommend this *let go* mentality whenever the going gets particularly tough.

## CLOSING THOUGHTS ON DRIVING

Some of the best ideas for driving are actually very simple. Stay relaxed and loose for extra control of the ball. For extra distance, tee it high. Maintain your grip pressure (fairly light) from address all the way to finish. Make a balanced swing, and sense that the fastest part of your golf swing is past the ball. Visualize your favorite hole or a beautiful flight of your upcoming shot, trust your swing, and let go.

## DRILLS TO IMPROVE YOUR DRIVING

*Train Your Right Side.* Practice a natural side-arm tossing motion with your right arm. Practice the correct positions in the eight steps by swinging a club with your right hand and arm only. I've watched Nick Price hit 240 yard 3 woods off the ground at my golf school range at Doral.

Put the clubshaft on your neck. Stick your finish like a pro.

*Play Tee-ball Golf.* When you can—perhaps in the early evening—play nine holes alone. Hit ten drives off each tee, then go to the next hole. Assuming the nine has two par-3 holes, you will be hitting seventy driver shots to actual landing areas of regulation holes. Keep track of the number of fairways you hit.

*Drag the Clubhead.* Gardner Dickinson, a legendary player and teacher, devised a drill that helps you swing in such a way that the clubhead approaches the ball on a shallower angle, facilitating solid contact. For good players, this drill produces the feeling of taking the hands out of the swing. Address an imaginary ball and take your normal stance, but set the clubhead down even with your right foot. Make sure the clubhead is inside the target line and the clubface is open. Now drag the clubhead forward through the imaginary ball, making a conscious effort to close the clubface—to square the toe through impact. On the follow-through, the toe of the clubface should point skyward. Continue through to a full, balanced finish, extending your right arm while the left arm folds at the elbow. This will give you the sensation of the no-hands release, the body and the club working together, and shallower angle of approach through impact and into the finish position.

*Sweep the Ball Drill.* I've used this, and it has been a lifesaver drill for good players who experience a severe driving slump. It teaches many of the fundamentals seen in great drivers. I developed this drill for a young bag room assistant working for me at Quaker Ridge Golf Club in Scarsdale, New York. He was about the worst driver I had ever seen. I gave him a drill to practice over the winter, designed to create a sweeping through the hitting area, and he did it over and over. The next summer he was 100 percent improved. He moved up to assistant pro and shot a 65 at Quaker Ridge, a very difficult course designed by A. W. Tillinghast.

To do the drill, use a fairway wood with generous loft. Tee the ball one inch off the ground. Address the ball as you normally would, but keep the left arm limp and tension free. Now swing back with what feels like a half back-swing, at about 60 percent of full force. Because the club and arms never get high in the backswing, you cannot swing along a steep incline.

Initiate the change of direction from backswing to forward swing *from the ground up*. The clubhead will be only about shoulder high in the back-swing as you initiate the forward motion. Feel your feet, knees, and hips shift laterally. This lateral movement should occur before the clubhead has completed its backward arc. Once it's triggered, the clubshaft will fall into the slot (i.e., approach the ball from an inside and shallow "attack track"), wrist cock will increase, the right elbow will start down toward the ball, the width of the swing will narrow dramatically from the backswing to the forward swing, and you will sense an *out-in* or *wide-to-narrow action*.

As you swing through the ball fully, make a "no-hands" release and keep your left wrist solid. Allow your left elbow to fold after impact and your right arm to elongate. If you made no effort to swing with your hands, you'll feel the club sweeping powerfully through the ball, with the ball staying on the clubface longer at impact. You'll also feel your hands and arms coming up in front of your chest, which is a good sign. It is truly an awesome feeling to experience.

The shot you will hit is a low, line-drive draw, the draw coming not from flipping the hands but instead from "firing" your entire right side. One final point to check on your no-hands back-and-through swing: look for the toe of the club to be up on both sides of the swing.

Remember—it's a mini-swing drill, with the purpose being to deliver a shallow arc. You should try for shots of only one hundred fifty to two hundred yards, nothing near full power. The small swing done correctly will give you incredible distance—much more than expected.

*The Red Dot Drill.* I have a red dot painted at the upper corner of my teaching bay. It is at the top of the wall, at the seam of the ceiling. From the mat in my bay, that red dot becomes a perfect aiming point for a three-quarter finish. The right arm and clubshaft should point closely to the red dot. Often the feeling my students have is an exaggerated sense of swinging left. It's like opening a pair of scissors, a separation. The club swings left, and the golf ball goes straight. Trying to hit that red dot really helps!

*Hit Drives between Flagpoles.* On the range, pick out a twenty-five-yard-wide landing area, then hit drives into the gap between two real or imaginary flagpoles. Keep track of your success rate whenever you do this. I recommend that you hit twenty drives, keeping track of how many "fairways" you hit. Do this drill for ten or more sessions, with the goal of moving your percentages up (15 out of 20 is excellent).

## JIM McLEAN'S TIP SHEET FOR GOOD DRIVING

### On the Tee, You Should

- Fundamental Number One: Strive for solid contact and center hits.
- Use a driver that is aesthetically pleasing to the eye and features the correct loft, lie, and shaft flex for you. Trying different drivers while getting readings from modern launch monitors can aid greatly in the correct fit.
- Adhere to a confident preshot routine.

- Love the challenge of driving the ball powerfully and accurately.
- Think positively.
- Play a shot—either a fade or a draw.
- Relax your grip pressure when you set up.
- Soften your arms and keep your wrists flexible at address.
- Feel and sense the center of your body in the swing.
- Connect your arm swing to the rotation of your body.
- Employ good footwork, rolling off the instep of each foot.
- Make your right shoulder, right hip, and right knee finish past the centerline of your body that is first established at address.
- Drive the ball through an imaginary window, positioned ten feet out in front of you, along the target line.
- Let your hipline rise through impact for more power

## Great Drivers

1. Visualize the optimum shot.
2. Don't freeze over the ball; stay in motion before pulling the trigger.
3. Let go.
4. Have two pivot points (the two legs) in their swings.
5. Have a shallow angle of attack.
6. Have a long flat spot in their swings.
7. Hit past the ball.
8. Go to a full finish position.
9. Have an athletic motion.
10. Swing within themselves.
11. Have extra power in reserve.

# THE RIGHT MINDSET

*Confusion Can Open the Door to Discovery*

Improving your golf game is a mental, physical, and some would say spiritual

quest. It's a wonderful, worthy endeavor, but it comes a lot easier to someone

who can handle momentary confusion. You see, in golf, confusion is some-

times necessary. Rather than something to avoid, confusion in the learning

process is actually something to welcome. Confusion indicates to me that a

student is truly thinking or feeling in a new way. If you think of confusion in

this manner, it can open your mind.

In plain fact, any time you take a formal lesson from a professional, try a tip from a golf magazine, or attempt to change your golf game in any way, you're likely to become slightly confused. Whatever the change, be it a theory, a drill, or an idea, it should result in a new "feel." This change in feel, this departure from your normal technique, is what triggers mental confusion. But confusion can be a good thing and a very normal part of the learning process. In fact, confusion can actually open the door to discovering new ways to swing and play better golf.

The best way to handle confusion is to see past it to the new understanding that awaits you. As you work through changes in your mind and body, you should welcome feeling new sensations involved in the swing, even though you aren't quite sure where each one will take you. If, in the end, these new elements of change don't feel good or fail to help you swing better, you can always go back to where you were before, knowing at the very least that you gained by learning what doesn't work for you. This is assuming you do not stick with some wild miracle method for too long, or fry your mind with too much detail, or continually jump from one instructor to another.

The alternatives to the improvement quest are giving up completely on new thoughts, or deciding that you are satisfied with where you are. In either case, you stop learning. In this way, you admit that either you've "got it," or that you never had all the answers anyway and are satisfied with the golf skills and ideas you have. No problem with this, except that I find many golfers are naturally curious and do possess an inner desire to excel. A substantial number of people will resist all change; yet, we know that change is the only thing that brings about progress for someone making fundamental mistakes. *Hard work and repetition of the same old wrong techniques is not the path to mastery.*

The swing is vastly complex, and there are many ways to attain excellent results. Jackie Burke, Ken Venturi, Harry "Lighthorse" Cooper, Claude Harmon, Carl Welty, Bob Toski, and all the greatest mentors in my life taught that there is constant learning, adjusting, and improving for all the better players. Many paths can be taken, and many will allow you to reach a satisfactory destination.

However, now is a good time to sound a warning: An abundance of what is written on the golf swing is controversial and contradicts other expert views, point by point. Mixing ideas from totally different concepts can be frustrating and is usually counterproductive. Without any doubt, there is a ton of misleading advice that I find fundamentally incorrect. Many very poor methods are advertised and heavily promoted with fantastic claims. They may well be teaching things that virtually no top players use. Going down one of these paths will lead to disastrous confusion and worse golf.

An interesting situation arises when a pure "method" teacher meets a student who believes *completely* in the method being taught and is physically adaptable to it. At that point, the golfer becomes a disciple. *He or she accepts absolute statements about the golf swing the way zealots accept their religious tenets.* The human mind is so strong that total belief in a teacher's method literally makes things happen. Thus, the student reaches a high level of mental clarity and focus. If the method is sound, the result can be that an average golfer becomes good and a good golfer becomes great. One very important part of the Eight-Step Swing system is its adaptability to any sound method. It is only a matter of matching up the key points of the method that an experienced teacher is trained to achieve.

Having said this, I'm truly convinced that the best method in the world cannot suit every golfer or even most golfers. The game and the swing are too individualized to allow for a series of absolutes. As I see it, there can be no unquestionably "correct way" to teach every player. Pure "method instructors" who become confident that they have seen it all and learned it all have probably just stopped noticing new things and have begun looking only for what they want to see. Students who never experience even a moment of confusion are either vastly brilliant or closed-minded.

On the driving range, most of you have experienced that odd feeling of hitting virtually every shot exactly as you want, to the point where you decide to experiment. You ask yourself, "Can I switch to a different swing action or swing thought and still get excellent results?" or "Now that I'm hitting the ball on the exact line as planned, can I stretch out the shot and get better distance?" Often, of course, this questioning process breaks the spell that produced all the good shots, but I wouldn't be too quick to criticize you for being inquisitive. Golf is such a demanding quest. We can't seem to stop searching, even when our goals are temporarily reached. We all tend to want just a little bit more. As the great Jackie Burke always said to me, "Golf is a game of upgrading." I believe this is a huge part of why the great Tiger Woods experiments so much and continues to search for a better way. Even as the dominant player and clearly Number One in the world, Tiger has continued his quest to get even better.

Ironically, when you have something that works, it is not a sure indication that this is the only answer. It doesn't mean that another approach will not work or that trying a new approach won't produce better results or a more interesting experience.

However, be careful not to become too much of a technical perfectionist, or you'll experiment forever and forget how to play the game. Seek to *crystallize* your concept of what you are doing, bearing in mind that the key points within that concept will change and develop and, one hopes, improve your game even more. I tell some of my students that it may actually be better for them to accentuate their uniqueness, rather than try to swing like everyone else. Difference is one definition of greatness, is it not?

Great athletes all use divergent ideas and techniques to perform at their peak levels. Consider, for example, the varying techniques of Ben Hogan, Jack Nicklaus, Lee Trevino, Fred Couples, Corey Pavin, Henrik Stenson, Lorena Ochoa, Annika Sorenstam, Morgan Pressel, Ryan Moore, Phil Mickelson, Ray Floyd, Lanny Wadkins, John Daly, Bruce Lietzke, Curtis Strange, Jim Furyk, and Sergio Garcia.

*Belief in yourself is the key ingredient to greatness.* "Belief is durable" the saying goes, and in golf that means trusting your system, your swing method, and your style of play. It is difficult or even impossible to alter a person's deeper beliefs; this is a simple fact. Over time, however, beliefs can change. For example, some of my teenaged thoughts about the golf swing now seem ridiculous to me. I remember that when my boys were three and four years old, they believed with all their hearts that a monster lived in the closet. Believing does not, in the end, make something true. But remember—beliefs are very powerful; in fact, there may not be anything more powerful than 100 percent belief.

Another axiom to consider: "It is better to travel hopefully than to arrive." But sometimes we do arrive. If, in your quest, you have used a drill to work toward a certain feeling and you get that result, it's time to put aside the drill. Come back to the drill if the fundamentals it has helped you refine begin to break down, but know when to stop.

The bottom line is that only one person can make you great. That person is you, not some teacher. Teachers, books, and methods can provide only limited assistance and guidance. *You alone must do the work and pay the price through hard, honest practice. You alone must be able to withstand pressure and hit the shots on the most solitary stage of all—the golf course.* The quest is similar from golfer to golfer, but there are many paths to choose from. *Doing it one's own way (with or without an instructor's help) is the most reliable producer of champions. To believe in yourself is to have power, whereas conforming to the current norms will almost always create mediocrity, leaving you just short of your personal best and far short of brilliance.* Only you can make the choice as to what physical skills and drills you will use to become a total player. *The interesting outcome is that, at a certain advanced stage of play, the game of golf becomes almost totally mental.*

# 12

# THE GREAT LEARNER

*Observations on How the Top Tour Pros Practice*

**QUALITY STUDENTS**

1. Listen intently
2. Clarify problems
3. Ask questions
4. Don't expect immediate results
5. Persevere
6. Are determined to succeed
7. Trust the teacher
8. Don't complain about minor setbacks
9. Follow the game plan devised with their teacher
10. Write down swing "thoughts" and "feels"
11. Set reachable goals within a set time frame
12. Don't always judge their progress by ball flight

Having been lucky enough to work with many top tour pros, I would like to give you some of my observations about one of their most important skills—the ability to learn and improve. I'll start with a story about a pro who was certainly one of the greatest students, learners, and practicers since Ben Hogan—Tom Kite.

At Doral, in 1992, I was working very hard with Kite on several difficult swing changes. Knowing Kite, I told him exactly what I thought about the status of his technique. That is what he always wants from me. He determined that what I told him was correct, so we set about making the changes on Tuesday of tournament week.

Now, understand that when Kite works on something he puts 100 percent effort into it. We continued the work we had done all year on the backswing, but we made a more dramatic change in his follow-through, which was geared to altering his swing path through impact. We taped it, reviewed it, hit balls again, retaped, reviewed again, and again, and again. This despite the fact that the Doral tour event began in just two days. We worked from dawn to after dusk, hitting balls in my Doral Superstation with the lights on long after dark. It was the same on Wednesday, except for the time when he was playing the Pro-Am.

All too soon, it was Thursday, tournament time, and Tom was headed to the first tee. I was busy teaching, so one of my instructors followed Kite on the first three holes that morning, and it wasn't pretty. He came back and told me that Tom had hit the worst snap hook ever into a lake about a hundred and fifty yards off the third tee—and this came after a five, five start. Needless to say, my heart sank. Could I have ruined Kite? Was he on his way to his highest score of the year?

About four hours later, Kite walked onto the practice tee at the golf school, and I went over to meet him. Not knowing what he had shot, I simply asked him (with my heart in my throat). Thankfully, it was seventy-three. Next, I asked him how he had hit the ball. Kite said he had started weak but later had hit some excellent shots. I then said, "I heard about the drive on number three—did you just forget about what we were working on after that and get back to something you could play with to get it around for today?"

I was a little taken back by Kite's response: "What do you mean, Jim?"

So I had to start over. "Well, did you go back to some old ideas?"

Tom looked at me as if I were crazy. He said forcefully, "Jim, I made a few bad swings out there, but the thought of changing never occurred to me. I *know* we are working on the right things. I don't care how I hit it today—I'm going to make the corrections necessary for the future."

That was the end of the conversation. We went right back to working on *the same things*.

Incidentally, in the final round on Sunday, Tom hit every fairway with his driver and all eighteen greens in regulation. He shot 65, 69 on the weekend to finish sixth. He came down to the Learning Center all pumped up and told me it was the best ball-striking round he had experienced in years. One month later he won at Atlanta, and soon after he captured the U.S. Open at Pebble Beach. The night after his win, I had a very special dinner in New York with just Tom Kite, Ben Crenshaw, and myself.

Through the 1990s I was struck by the work ethic of Tiger Woods. He continues to do the same in the new century. Yes, he is incredibly talented, but what truly sets him apart is his unquenchable desire to keep getting better. Tiger really does outwork everyone. Though he is gifted enough to be the best with a more normal effort, Tiger relentlessly pursues constant improvement.

Tiger's swing coach from 1997 to 2002, Butch Harmon, is a good friend of mine. We have worked together often, and our teaching styles are similar. Both of us believe in proven fundamentals, and we know that teaching golf is a moving target with every student. Not only is the goal to change for the better, but the game "feels" slightly different to even the best golfers every day. I believe Tiger Woods understands this perfectly. It allowed him to trust Butch and not blame the coach when he had an off week. Instead, he went right back to work on the fundamentals.

It should reassure all of us that even Tiger Woods still takes lessons and occasionally gets confused or has a bad day. It's important to realize that Woods always keeps his enthusiasm and his spirit. He is not about to give up or get down for too long. Instead, you'll find him out on the range or practicing his swing in front of a mirror. Despite being the Number One player in the world, Woods still gets excited about hitting a perfect shot, and his enthusiasm for the game only grows. Tiger exemplifies anyone who masters his craft. There is a big difference between someone who truly does the work to achieve high goals and someone who only thinks about it. There is a big difference between study and scholarship; take it from someone who has spent months, years, and decades breaking the rocks with a hammer. It's a continuous level of effort on solid fundamentals that gives you high achievement. This is true not only in golf but in all arts and sciences. Those who do not understand this will never understand this. They will never understand the great learner. Those who know, will know.

I once watched another Number One–ranked player and extremely hard worker—Nick Faldo—do something very interesting on the range. He was practicing drivers and hitting bullets. One after another seemed perfect. Then Faldo stepped away and talked with his teacher. He made a few practice swings and worked on a new little move. When he hit the next practice drive, he hit another bullet, except that this one carried about ten yards longer. A broad smile came across Nick's face, and he actually started doing a little dance. The thought occurred to me: Here is the Number One player in the world as excited about a great practice-range drive as any young teenager might be smoking a long, straight tee shot. Maybe more excited!

There is a big lesson here. *Appreciate the brilliant shots you hit. Give yourself credit. Remember your good shots and make them important—even on the practice tee.* Most golfers do just the opposite. They make a big deal about the bad shots, throwing clubs or criticizing themselves unmercifully. Don't. Take a lesson from the world's greatest students. Woods, Faldo, and Kite play golf because they love it. To them it is *art*. They paint pictures with their clubs. They can't wait for the next day of golf. Great students love the game.

# 13

# HOW TO PREPARE

*Establishing a Good Battle Plan*

*"The general who wins a battle makes many calculations in his temple before the battle is fought."*

—SUN TZU, *THE ART OF WAR*

Golfers who like to compete do not like to approach a tournament without being fully prepared. But honestly, what percentage of the time can you expect to bring your A game into competition? Usually there is some facet—perhaps your driver, or your putter, or your short iron game—that is not at its sharpest.

If that's the bad news, then the good news is this: no matter how well or poorly you are playing, no matter what your realistic chances are of winning the tournament, you can always win what I call the "four battles." By being totally prepared in these four areas, you will be near or at your best for any important event you enter.

Credit for this proven concept of establishing a competitive golf "battle plan" goes to Coach Jim Young and the Performance Institute of the Academy at West Point. The Army has a tremendous tradition of highly disciplined teams, and it's no accident that Vince Lombardi, Bobby Knight, Mike Krzyzewski, Al Davis, and Bill Parcells all at one time coached at West Point. Coach Young told me that there were five contests within every game that his Army varsity football team could win. Army was usually outmanned by bigger programs, but even if they were playing Number One–ranked Notre Dame, Young's philosophy was that the team could still win individual aspects of the game, which could, in the end, lead to victory or at least a highly competitive game.

I wondered if I could apply this same thinking to golf. Eventually I came up with the following four-point battle plan, designed to help you perform more proficiently under pressure. By the way, Tiger Woods applies the "four battles" to every event he enters. When Tiger said in the press that he won with his "C game," he took a lot of criticism for being too cocky. The truth is that Tiger has won many tour events with far less than his A game. Here is how you can get the most out of the game you bring to the course.

## BATTLE NUMBER ONE

*WIN the Pretournament Battle.* To win the pretournament battle, you must begin your preparation for the tournament well in advance. Finish up projects that have been hanging. Get to all those important phone calls to business associates and family. Go to the eye doctor, the dentist, the chiropractor.

"Clear your desk," and then begin your homework on the golf course you'll be playing. Even if you've played it many times, walk it with a notepad and pencil. Determine where you want to hit the ball, then locate the "bailout" spots where you wouldn't mind seeing your mis-hit shots land. Where there's a layup shot facing you, plan that layup shot down to the last little bounce, with a plan to land the ball a specific distance from the pin. Be sure you know exactly how far you are hitting your wedges. Finally, carefully analyze your golf game. Determine what area of your game needs the most work, and get to it. (Always spend some extra time before any event working on putting and chipping.) The object is to begin all your tournament preparations well in advance.

## BATTLE NUMBER TWO

*WIN the Preround Battle.* Start by getting your equipment in perfect order. Make sure every grip is clean and tacky; every groove on every iron is scraped clean; your golf balls are marked for identification; your shoes are re-spiked; and you have extra gloves, sweater, sunscreen, lip balm, water jug, lucky socks, and whatever you could possibly think of later so you don't say, "I wish I'd brought my—"

Then, every day of the event, block out a generous amount of time between your departure for the course and your tee time. Know exactly how long it takes to get to the golf course, and then give yourself twice that amount of time. I remember the first time I saw Lee Trevino in the locker room at Sleepy Hollow Country Club in Scarborough, New York, several hours before his tee time for the PGA Senior Tour Commemorative. I asked him why he was so early, and he explained to me his routine. If Trevino hits traffic, needs gas, has a flat tire, or takes a wrong turn, he never has to worry, because he factors these long-shot possibilities into his schedule. Trevino can always be found in the locker room well before his scheduled tee time in a tournament, doing what some people would call wasting time. True, he is talking, resting, or just hanging out—but he's not wasting time. He's preparing to win a golf tournament, and he knows that to play his best he has to have some down time for all the essentials of travel, getting dressed, eating, and hitting practice shots. By arriving extra early, Lee knows he will walk out of that locker room for his pre-round practice exactly on time. The point is to leave nothing to chance and to remove completely the possibility of feeling rushed.

You *can't* control how the wind blows, so concentrate on the things you can control, one of which is remembering to check the wind direction before teeing off and to anticipate how and which way it will be blowing on every

Lee Trevino's practice sessions are a vital part of his preround battle plan.

hole. Usually, there is a flag near the clubhouse that will help with this deter-mination. Remember that on the course the wind may be swirling through different areas and can fool you if you are not truly aware of the general direc-tion. Some top tour players draw a wind direction line on every hole in their yardage book prior to teeing off. The reason is that on the golf course and in protected areas, it is easy to lose a good sense of wind direction.

Go through your warm-up routine in exactly the way that makes you feel most comfortable. *I recommend beginning the day by practice putting and then going to the driving range to warm up the full swing.* I feel that those warm-up putts are quite important (especially some long lag putts) to establish the green speed and your "feel" for the day. Finish your warm-up session using the club you will hit off the first tee. Rehearse that shot in detail, and you will feel much more relaxed heading to the first tee. Allow extra time to reach the tee. This will allow you to focus and prepare for your all-important first tee shot of the day.

## BATTLE NUMBER THREE

*WIN the Emotional Battle.* Entire books are written about the emotional and mental approach to sports, including golf. You should know the mental/emotional state that allows you to perform at your best. The one tip I would add is this: before you tee off, it is often helpful to realize that every round usually has bogeys in it. The thing is, we don't know where, when, or if they will come. Many fine rounds have early bogeys, sometimes two in a row. Promise yourself that if you bogey hole one and hole two, you will visualize your scorecard with those bogeys isolated among a long string of pars. Re-member that scoring bogeys on holes one and two is not a sure sign of your worst round. On the other hand, if you start out with two birdies, the reverse is true. It does not mean you should do anything different. Stick to your game plan, and do not project results. Continue your shot-by-shot mentality. Stay in the present tense. Accept your success without taking on any doubts or unreal responsibilities to shoot a record score.

Winning the emotional battle will be more difficult on certain days. However, this remains a battle that you are capable of winning every time, provided you maintain your composure, even when you swing poorly or don't score to the best of your abilities on a particular hole or several holes. You can still have the best attitude of anyone playing this event.

Anger usually brings mistakes that add strokes to your score. You then take needless risks, and your score gets worse. That is why it's extremely important to stay mentally level and focused. Sure, I know it's easy to get upset in golf. The irony is, in some cases that anger can be helpful in snapping you out of a funk. I think any good golfer is going to be angry with a bad shot. The key is to get over it. Earl Woods taught his son the "ten-step rule." He told Tiger to go ahead and get mad, but after he took ten steps, to let it go. Excellent advice. If you go into each round knowing that luck is involved and that every shot you hit will not be your best, then attitude problems can be greatly reduced.

I find it very useful to have students keep things in perspective. We would all do well to play golf shot by shot or hole by hole, and leave each hole behind as we move to the next. So many of us play golf in the past or in the future when we really need to play in the present.

Jackie Burke always told the University of Houston golf team to focus on the performance at hand and to forget about results. Burke taught me many vital lessons about golf during my college days, but none was more important than his two-sided formula: P/R=$, whereas R/P=0. Translation: *performance over results leads to success, whereas emphasizing results over performance leads to failure.*

It's okay to form a result-oriented goal. But if you are result conscious while you are performing, if you think ahead while there are shots still to be hit, you may not be able to take care of the shot at hand. Your mind will be distracted from the present, and your performance will not be 100 percent. Living in the future or the past is not the optimal performance state. It is a distraction. Take care of the shot at hand, and those coveted good results will happen. *Performance first—always.*

## Focus on Your Performance!

$$\frac{P}{R} = \$$$

$$\frac{R}{P} = 0$$

## BATTLE NUMBER FOUR

*WIN the Management Battle.* Before you tee off, eat and drink what you need to avoid mental or physical fatigue. I notice that almost every professional golfer keeps a power bar, a banana, or a sandwich in the golf bag to eat during the round. You should also get plenty of water during the round. Then once you begin your round, you will stay mentally connected to the golf course and how it's playing, especially with regard to wind, moisture, dryness, mowing, watering, etc. Promise yourself that you won't get caught on a tee without the right club because you let the caddie walk ahead or you parked the cart too far away. Promise yourself that you will follow a set game plan that involves not taking unrealistic risks. Between shots, relax and pace yourself. Do not try to concentrate intensely for the full duration of the round.

Winning the management battle requires that you fairly assess your strengths and weaknesses and then maximize your strengths. Good course managers do not make dumb mistakes. I keep a saying on my teaching bays from the great football coach Bill Parcells: "Dumb players do dumb things." The inverse is that smart players do smart things, so try to be a smart golfer if you want to shoot lower scores. Good players are aware of everything and miss nothing. They can "zone out" distractions. They plan and "see" each shot. Currently, Tiger Woods displays tremendous management skills and is a great model.

As I continue to repeat, golf is a game of adjustments, and usually the player who makes the fewest and the least costly mistakes will remain in the game with a good chance to win. Whatever physical mistakes you commit in competition, you should be able to contain them and move on if your preparation is thorough and if you make sure to control everything that's controllable.

I believe that it's possible for you to win all four of these battles. Try, and you will give yourself the best opportunity to compete at your optimum level, time and time again.

How many golfers do you know whose swings are far short of classic? Who don't get much distance on their drives? Who play a slice with every club but the short irons? And who, despite these shortcomings, post impressive scores and often win the "Nassau" bet? These are the golfers who know themselves and know their games, who play within themselves and are good course managers. As John Wooden once said, "Don't let what you cannot do interfere with what you can do."

*"Plan conservatively. Execute aggressively."*

—BOB ROTELLA, SPORTS PSYCHOLOGIST

To make sure we distribute the satisfaction these golfers feel more widely among the population, *teachers must begin emphasizing course management so that students understand that management skills depend on how well they know themselves and their game and how well they translate this knowledge into a sound plan by which to play each hole.* At our golf schools, we get our students on the golf course as much as possible.

When sports psychology experts like Dick Coop, Bob Rotella, Fran Piroz-zolo, Lanny Bassham, and Chuck Hogan discuss the mental side of golf, they never stray far from the principle of *self-knowledge*. Of all games, golf exposes fraud and self-delusion most efficiently. There is no other sport, besides perhaps the high jump, in which the task at hand is so obvious. In effect, we golfers call our shots every time we come to bat. When we select a three-wood trying to reach a par-5 green protected by water some two hundred and fifty yards away, we are in effect pointing to the center field bleachers. Likewise, if we can plan the golf equivalent of a walk, a hit-and-run single, or a squeeze bunt and still make birdie, we've succeeded just as well. If you are not in touch with your own ability and your own golf psyche, your competitors will know that soon enough—whatever kind of player you are.

In the past few years, CBS's Gary McCord and other TV golf announcers have described many a successful golf shot by saying "good play." This phrase has always been appropriate to sports in which the athlete must react to a situation, such as when a shortstop charges a slow roller and throws home, or a point guard hits the open player underneath for a layup. But in golf, with a ball and a target that don't move, does it make sense to say "good play"? The answer is yes, absolutely. The key is not whether things are moving or standing still; it's whether or not there are options and choices. Like the shortstop and the point guard, the golfer has options. He or she has more time to think but also has a greater number of options on most shots. When tour players assess the lie, the score they need to make, the strengths and weaknesses of their game, and where their competition stands, they are reacting to a situation. If they read the situation improperly, they can make a shot correctly but still get in trouble. When they devise a plan—from club selection, to swing technique, to the shape of the shot—and go on to execute it, the two words they are truly hoping to hear from the caddie are *good play*.

Most of us make good plays when we are at peace with ourselves and feel an inward calm. Here are two proven ways to achieve a golf state of mind that will enhance your performance.

- **Assess the game you've brought to the course that day.** Once you take an honest account of the current state of your golf skills (as this changes every day), you are ready to establish a game plan based on shots you are comfortable executing, as opposed to shots you can only hope to hit. For each hole, you should have a plan based on shots that you have at least a 50 percent chance for success with, but a 70 to 80 percent chance for success should be the norm.

- **Commit yourself to target golf.** Good course management is a matter of *targets and plans*. From the first swing on the first tee until the final putt on hole number eighteen, you will do nothing but define your targets and plan realistic ways to reach them. Obviously, no plan works perfectly; that's why it's called a plan. There will almost always be shots that stray from the plan and miss the target by a substantial margin. When this happens, you play a recovery shot that permits you to get back to your game plan as soon as possible. The other option is mentally to beat yourself up for failing to execute, and that's the classic mental Death Move. Even on recovery shots, you are still dealing with a target and a plan—you hope a very reasonable one. Dr. Pirozzolo says to commit 100 percent to every shot, and then use 80 percent effort to execute the shot. You do not get a peak performance by overtrying. Keep something in reserve. This will help you relax and execute under pressure. Being aware of targets throughout your round of golf—as opposed to being totally preoccupied with hitting the ball—is a big step for a golfer. *It's the difference between "playing golf" and spending eighteen holes trying to "make golf swings."* Always ask yourself, "What am I trying to do?" I tell my students to actually answer that question. It's a mistake to blame the Execution Department for a major error made by the Planning Department.

## BASIC TIPS FOR GOOD COURSE MANAGEMENT

- **Stay focused.** Pay attention to what must be accomplished in the present. Tune out your three-putt on the last hole (the past). Forget the tough par-5 next hole (the future). The only important shot in the entire round is the present shot, which is the one you have to hit next.

- **Have confidence.** The attitude you must walk around with is one that has you believing you will successfully hit every shot as long as you stay focused. If you are playing within your capabilities, there is no reason to doubt your ability to execute the plan and hit your targets.

- **Relax.** Trying to make things happen, rather than staying relaxed and *letting them happen*, is the great builder of tension. Tension usually destroys the naturalness of your golf swing. If you feel tension building, concentrate on keeping your hands and arms soft—especially at address but all throughout the swing as well. Keep the hands and arms soft, and you dramatically increase your odds of making a good swing. *Perhaps the most important words in golf are these: "Let go or Let it happen."* I played many rounds of tournament golf with the great Canadian golfer Moe Norman. Moe, who is considered one of the top ball strikers of all time, would often tell me that the three most important words in the English language were "to let go." It's okay to be nervous—even scared—at times. However, you can and you must find a way to relax your hands and arms.

- **Hit through the window.** Any time a golfer conducts a complete analysis of the shot that must be played, there is the possibility that he or she eventually begins seeing everything that could go wrong. In a pressure situation, you may be wise to assess your situation fairly quickly, keeping most of your preshot focus on the good, smooth swing you want to make. Stand behind your ball, then pick an aiming point about ten feet ahead of the ball, imagining that it is a suspended open window at the height you desire. This window image will reduce your peripheral sight and help you concentrate on the swing. Now just hit the ball through the window. Even if it is not a perfect shot, the ball will likely start on line. If there were a window out in front of you on every shot, you would accelerate the club through the ball at a good speed and hit many more good shots per round. Again, avoid taking too much time analyzing, and avoid thoughts of where not to hit the ball. This is a mental tip I gave the great New York amateur, George Zahringer. It was an idea he used constantly as he won national events and dominated amateur golf in the metropolitan area. It is also one of the best articles I ever did for *Golf Digest* based on all the people who thanked me for writing it.

- **"If I don't hit a good shot . . ."** Let's face it: many golfers put far too much pressure on themselves. Trying for perfection can be dangerous. No one is perfect, and golf will always be a game of misses—for the good course manager, playable misses. Sometimes not trying so hard is a big tension reliever. An example could be on a crucial four-foot putt. Instead of thinking, "I must hole this putt," try telling yourself, "If I don't hole this putt, so what." No one will put you in front of a firing squad. You'll be surprised how many putts you will make. With an effort level set much lower, try this same strategy in any other pressure-filled shot-making situation.

- **Keeping score.** There is an alternative approach to scorekeeping that for some of my students has changed their entire outlook on playing a round of golf. Instead of reporting the results of each hole in strict numerical terms, this kind of scorekeeping gives the shot-by-shot record of a given round. It lists fairways hit, greens hit in regulation, bunker saves, total number of putts, etc. You can play a point game for each fairway hit and each green hit in regulation. Try to achieve a target score. This takes your mind off the score.

Improvement in these various aspects of golf is another true indication of progress, and defining your day of golf in this way also makes you a much better course manager. When golfers concentrate on these *shot-by-shot* challenges, they stop putting themselves down for the few bad shots they hit. Over time, the alternative scorecards provide an excellent readout of strengths and weaknesses, which means that practice time can be budgeted all the more effectively.

## NOTES ON PHYSICAL FITNESS

The importance placed upon fitness and physical conditioning has increased for tour players and the general golf world over recent years, for several reasons. Top players are training with fitness experts who have shown that improved physical conditioning (posture, flexibility, stability, strength, and power) can enhance performance.

Golfers traditionally have been slow to accept these truths, but this is changing rapidly. As the general public bears witness to the fact that physical conditioning enhances the level of play for top golfers such as Tiger Woods, they are coming to accept the benefits of physical conditioning and resistance training for better golf.

Experts in biomechanics, athletic development, sports medicine, and physical therapy continue to educate the public on the benefits of stretching, resistance training, and aerobic exercise for better golf performance. Exercise can improve not only a person's enjoyment of the game but their quality of life as well.

Finally the world of golf instruction is coming to the realization that a golfer may have certain physical limitations, such as previous injuries, muscle or joint inflexibility, muscular weaknesses, or imbalances, that prevent them from executing the desired swing mechanics. Employing the science of biomechanics at our golf schools, with the assistance of Dr. Robert Neal, has added a new dimension to our teaching and golf instruction.

The reason we introduced a sports biomechanist to our organization was to assist our understanding of the cause-and-effect relationships that determine human motion in a sports context. By definition, biomechanics applies the laws of mechanics and physics to human motion or performance—in our case golf performance.

By using three-dimensional golf swing analysis in our golf schools, we now have a quantitative measure of exactly what our golfer does during the swing. This very accurate dynamic assessment of their swing mechanics can also give us valuable insights into their physical capabilities. Information about body positions at various points during the swing, body speeds, and efficiency (timing or kinematic sequencing) measures, combined with physical screening tests, allows us to make important decisions about their technical path to improvement. For instance, if we discover that our golfer is lacking flexibility in trunk rotation, their ability to generate power in the golf swing may be hampered, and our ability to make technical changes to address that deficiency may be somewhat limited as a result. Thus, a course of stretching to improve trunk rotational flexibility may be prescribed so that the technical change can take place. Obviously, most amateur golfers do not have access to high-tech biomechanics or experts in fitness. However, you do have great access to information on the Internet. You can also find locations where you can get expert advice. My advice is to use trainers who are familiar with golf technique.

Several important aspects of physical conditioning apply to improving a student's game. Combined stretching and resistance training improves the flexibility, range of motion, stability, and strength in those areas of the body targeted by the exercises. Golfers rely heavily on the hips, spine, and shoulders to generate the energy in the swing, and on the joints of the upper limb, including the wrists, to transfer that energy to the club. When these areas are limited in their range of motion (i.e., the person has insufficient flexibility), a golfer's swing is certainly going to lack power and efficiency.

## Stretching

Stretching is a must for the average golfer, especially the senior golfer, who loses flexibility with the aging process. Thus, golfers who are serious about improving their game need to allocate time to golf-specific stretching routines. Similarly, by taking a few minutes to warm up before a practice session or round, a golfer is less likely to encounter injuries and will also improve the execution of their swing. A correct warm-up is not just a couple of quick stretches before hitting the first tee shot! Stretching after a round or practice is important, too, since it will lessen the likelihood of sore muscles and stiffness the following day.

## Resistance Training

Resistance training, if it is functional and challenging for the individual, is another form of exercise that can add not only to a person's strength but also to their dynamic flexibility. There was, and may still be, a misconception that lifting weights will bulk up a player and decrease his or her flexibility.

This notion is ill-founded, because research has shown that if resistance training is combined with flexibility exercises, the athlete increases both strength and flexibility. The program that a competitive golfer should follow is completely different from that of a body builder. Golfers should use all forms of resistance, including their own body weight, free weights (dumbbells and barbells), machines (e.g., rotational devices to improve trunk rotational strength), elastic bands, and medicine balls to promote strength and stability in a functional way. Strength conditioning can be used to improve the framework of a golfer—the legs, hips, abdominals, back, and shoulders—so that a player has a more stable base to work with. Many top players suffer from back problems because of weaknesses in these areas. The average player may find that strengthening the midsection improves coordination and sequence of movement, which is vital for creating clubhead speed. In fact, if you access a golf fitness specialist who is up-to-date with the field, activities or exercises that are prescribed to you will focus not just on increasing your strength but increasing it so that it is useable strength. That is, your exercises will emphasize speed, coordination, and segment sequencing, and that will be of huge benefit to your actual golf swing.

That does not mean, however, that *every* activity in your workout routine should mimic a golf swing. Quite the contrary! You need to progress from simple to complex movements as you gain the necessary stability, flexibility, and coordination required for the complex drills and exercises.

Many amateurs may actually benefit more from strengthening the shoulders, forearms, and wrists, since they most directly control the club and clubface. Most importantly, however, the serious golfer *must* develop a strong and stable lower body (gluteals, low back musculature, and lower abdominals), coupled with a strong upper back (shoulder blade stabilizing muscles, lower traps, lats, and so forth). The upper back muscles must be able to resist the inertia of the arms and club during the downswing as they try to "pull" the golfer toward the ball. Most women and junior golfers are not strong enough in the upper back, and this robs them of speed on the downswing and an inability to maintain a stable spine, about which the torso rotates.

The left arm for right-handed golfers needs to have the appropriate strength to strike the ball with a flat or slightly bowed wrist. Women are typically weaker than men in these areas and may see immediate improvement by doing strengthening exercises.

Strength conditioning alone may not improve a person's swing, but it may act as a catalyst for swing changes. In fact, just getting stronger alone does not mean that your swing mechanics will improve. You need high-quality instruction so that you can take advantage of your increased strength. However, by improving strength in certain areas, a golfer may trust a change or actually adopt a technique alteration more easily than if adequate strength is not present.

## Aerobic Exercise

Finally, aerobic exercise is another component of physical conditioning that improves a golfer's stamina and endurance. For the recreational player, aerobic exercise such as running, cycling, or swimming can trim the waistline. For the serious competitor, the benefits of aerobic exercise may show up more on the weekend days of a tournament, when a player's ability to avoid fatigue and stay mentally focused can lead to a top finish rather than a late fade. Vision, mental clarity, and physical endurance are all traits that can be associated with good physical well-being.

## A CLAUDE HARMON STORY ON HOW NOT TO PREPARE FOR A BIG EVENT

At the 1966 Masters, Claude arrived with his youngest son, Billy, then sixteen and making his first trip to Augusta. As a past champion, Claude drove to the front gate wearing his green coat and received a warm reception from the guard, who waved them on down the famed Magnolia Lane. Claude drove to the front of the clubhouse and was again warmly received. Billy took in everything and loved seeing the giant Masters trophy inscribed with his father's name. Next Claude suggested they head up to the Champions Locker Room. There Billy was introduced to several past champions. On their way out of the Champions Locker Room, they went through the regular locker room for a tour of the course, a young contestant recognized Claude and jumped off the bench he was sitting on. "Mr. Harmon, you don't know me, but I'm playing in my first Masters and I wanted to meet you," the amateur said.

Claude Harmon was old school, so he responded coolly to the brash kid. He quickly moved onward with Billy. In an effort to keep the conversation from ending, the amateur blurted out, "You know, Claude, I've been very surprised at Augusta. I'm surprised how easy this golf course is. I find it over-rated."

This stopped Claude in his tracks, he turned around, and he fixed the young man with a stare and came back sharply. "Son," he said, "I've never heard of you, but tomorrow is the first round of the Masters. You will realize that as you drive down Magnolia Lane—that's 2! You'll walk into the locker room and see the greatest players in the world like Nicklaus, Palmer, and Watson—that's 2 more! You'll walk out to the range and see the forty thousand spectators and all the scoreboards—that's another 2. You'll walk to the first tee, where they will slide your name into the starting slot—that's 2 more. You haven't even teed off yet, and I've already got you for 80!" With that, Claude turned and walked away, with a stunned Billy in tow. The next day, the chastened amateur found out that Mr. Harmon was correct. When the flag went up, the course got a whole lot tougher.

I've stood on that first tee at Augusta and hit my opening tee shot at the Masters. I know what it's like, and it's a lot different from what many teachers and golfers imagine. You'd better have trust, belief, and a golf swing you know. I'm quite certain that many club champions couldn't break 100 playing in the Masters, and I know for sure that many teachers expounding the miracle method they teach couldn't do it, either.

The point to Claude's story is that tournament golf is not what most people think. You truly have to be ready for any competitive round of golf. Having a technically perfect swing method will not take you very far if you do not have the right mind set and the confidence to let go.

Another lesson from the story: Don't make big proclamations before a tournament.

## SELF-MANAGEMENT

Choosing targets and devising plans for each shot is a constant mental—and emotional—challenge that requires true self-knowledge. Playing smart golf—doing all the little things that make the difference between shooting 100 or 88, 86 or 78, 74 or 68, losing a match or winning it—is to enjoy this game in the best way possible.

Unfortunately, the majority of golfers never fully recognize the importance of course management—which is really self-management. But for those who build up their mental technique and really learn to think their way around the golf course, the rewards include not just well-played golf but a larger understanding of themselves and the world around them.

# 14

# TEACHING GEMS

*Twenty-eight Short but Great Tips on the Golf Swing*

1. The golf swing moves in a circle—as viewed from *overhead! There are no straight lines. The clubhead orbits around you.* Get a visual picture of the perfect arc!

2. The big muscles of your body provide the extra power to accelerate the arms and the club. Learn a powerful athletic golf move by learning a power sequence.

3. Your arms guide the club on the plane:
   - The arms basically stay in front of the chest.
   - They respond to the motions of the body at the beginning of the downswing.
   - You can vary your arm action to shape all types of shots and trajectories.

4. Your hands are a primary source of information to the brain about what the clubhead and clubface are doing. The eyes are equally important.

- The hands are used to fine-tune the shot.
- It can be useful to think of the back of the left hand as having the same alignment as the clubface.
- You can do the same with the right hand. For example, you can "shake hands with the target" as you hit through the ball. This can be an excellent swing thought for many golfers.

5. Based on the amount of time you practice properly, major changes may take six months to a year.

6. You retain very little (about 5 percent) of what you hear. Most people learn much better through

- Demonstrations
- Pictures
- Training aids
- Drills
- Feeling the change (kinesthetics): a qualified teacher moving you or your golf club in a better way

7. If you are nonathletic you can become a good player, but you will require more attention, supervision, perseverance, and dedicated practice.

8. *Master the basics* is a great learning concept. I have a sign in our Superstation: "Be Brilliant at the Basics." Make sure you are a master of

- Alignments
- Grip pressure
- Balance, tempo, rhythm
- The finish

9. Mirrors are great coaches.

10. Most golfers are capable of getting better, but too rarely they actually

make decisions that give them a chance to improve. Most golfers jump from one idea to another and can never connect the dots.

11. *No tip* is correct for everyone. Every tip I have ever heard or read is correct for somebody at some time. Most tips you hear will not pertain to your swing.

12. To improve your golf swing, do the following:
    - Be willing to change.
    - Make a commitment to do what is necessary.
    - Schedule time to practice.
    - Be realistic about how long it takes for lasting improvement.
    - Believe in what you are doing.

13. "Practice" does not necessarily mean standing on the range banging balls hour after hour.

14. Proper use of your range time is an important part of improving. Make sure you are making the correct practice moves.

15. Many things can be improved upon and learned that *do not* require you to go to the range.

16. Change your target from time to time while on the practice range.

17. Do not practice longer than you can stay focused. If you can't concentrate, *quit*.

18. Rhythm, timing, and balance are important—very important.

19. Talent is God-given; technique can be learned.

20. Demanding that golf instruction be simple is a fallacy. The golf swing is a series of moves that are in fact not simple for most people. Incomplete instruction can take you only so far, and then it becomes ineffective. What a really good teacher can often do is make very simple points that are also very clear to the student. That is great teaching. This same teacher will continue to build a better swing piece by piece, a little at a time, simple point by simple point, clearly communicated. This *building-block approach* is how almost anyone can build a highly effective golf swing.

21. The first move away from the ball, early take-away, is highly underated by most teachers and most golfers.

22. A good golfer plans for success.

23. Tension kills the golf swing!

24. "Most shots are missed before you take the club away, at setup."—Ken Venturi

25. "Enthusiasm without truth equals frustration."—Dave Collins, Jim McLean Master Instructor

26. When a teacher writes a new miracle way to swing the golf club, it is probably nothing that has not been taught before. The "new method" is just packaged differently.

27. There is no one miracle swing method. If it were a miracle, don't you think the teacher teaching the method would be a fantastic player?

28. Practice your short game two days each month. Take an entire morning or afternoon to devote exclusively to short shots and putting. This will take strokes off your score, guaranteed.

# 15

# MASTERY

*It's the Journey, Not the Destination*

There's good practice and there's bad practice. In my regular lunch meetings

with Claude Harmon, he would often lament seeing frustrated golfers trying

to improve by mindlessly "beating balls." He'd tell the story of the man who

buys a Ferrari and excitedly heads out of Winged Foot Country Club from

Westchester County bound for New York City. He gets on I–95 but mistakenly

goes north instead of south. He puts the pedal to the floorboard and races

down the highway at over a hundred miles per hour. He's making great time, but he's got two serious problems: He's getting farther from New York City with every mile, and he's liable to kill himself in the process. Like the golfer beating balls with no clue, Claude would say, the man in the Ferrari lacks direction, and sadly he will never reach his destination.

That's bad practice. Good practice involves ingraining correct golf movements, the understanding of which begins in the intellect but must be transferred to the muscles through hitting balls and proper drills. People with superior physical aptitude will learn faster, but no one becomes an excellent golfer without paying the price on the "rock pile." For a fundamental change to occur in your swing, there must be sufficient time for the conscious and unconscious mind to accept it. My rule of thumb is to allow about one month of steady effort for the student to internalize one significant component of a swing change. Then he or she can go on to the next new move.

The player who works consistently on solid fundamentals and makes progress in small segments will tend not to lose overnight what he or she has gained over time. When the player does slide backward, the slide will be minor and the turnaround not long in the making. There are no shortcuts to the mastery of golf. Intelligent practice is the only way to narrow the gap between knowing something about the swing and employing it correctly.

I like to believe I have helped some players simply by changing their entire outlook on practice. Practice doesn't have to be just hitting balls down a driving range. It can be fun. It can be done in short sessions. It can take place at home or in your backyard, and it can be greatly enhanced if you adopt a positive attitude toward the game, read helpful books and articles, and study videotapes.

One interesting example along these lines occurred with Gary Player at my former Learning Center at Sleepy Hollow. During a practice session, I brought Gary inside to watch some particular video footage of Ben Hogan. There were two specific swings Hogan made that I knew Gary would love to see. Sure enough, he was tremendously interested. I replayed each swing hundreds of times, and we viewed the tape for more than two hours. Gary and I spent a great deal of time talking about what he saw and knew about Hogan.

After this in-depth viewing, Gary went back to the practice tee with more enthusiasm and a vivid picture of what I had seen in his swing. The next day he shot 66 in the Commemorative, then an event on the Champions Tour. Gary gave full credit to the Hogan swings that we watched together and that remained clearly in his mind. It led to a completely new feel and picture of what he wanted to do.

You are practicing whenever you repeat exercises and drills on a regular basis, no matter where you happen to be. Golfers who retool their full swings often wonder if they can improve by taking one or two lessons or whether they need a six-week or a twenty-week series. The number of formal lessons you take can be reduced significantly if you and your instructor can devise a detailed, comprehensive practice program that, incidentally, will involve doing swing drills without hitting balls.

Train your swing positions and movements with a weighted club.

Practicing with a weighted "doughnut" on your club helps you groove a good swing. Here the player is holding the correct delivery position.

Practice the Eight-Step Swing using a regular club, a swing fan, or a weighted club. It is very helpful to swing in front of a mirror, and I know this will work for you if you are diligent. You would also benefit by watching my DVD series titled, *The Building Block Approach*, featuring the eight steps. Put yourself in the correct positions (the positions you need to improve) and hold each one, over and over. The more repetitions the better. The more you practice in this way, the quicker your old habits and your old swing problems will melt away. Realize that changing a physical habit requires constant attention and repetition. I know one thing for sure: everyone is different. Some will change quickly; others will take much more time.

When you are on the range hitting balls, always execute a significant number of your shots using your full pre-shot routine. At least 20 percent of

Hitting to a target during practice will allow you to simulate the course situation.

your shots on the range should be hit following a full implementation of your pre-shot pattern. This is practicing as you would play. It adds a whole dimension to practice. Try to hit two of every ten shots using a target and a pre-shot routine. This way, your practice will simulate actual play, at least somewhat.

## THE RIGHT PRACTICE SWINGS

We've all heard the statement "My practice swing is great, but when I go to hit the ball my swing is terrible" groaned a thousand times. Has it ever struck you as somewhat illogical? It should. Most amateurs far overrate their practice swings.

Most people have the same body movements and swing mistakes in their practice swing as in their real swing. What changes is their *tempo* and the fact that they are not impacting an object. Because they swing slowly with no fear of mis-hitting the ball, their practice swing feels pretty good. Only it isn't. The same mistakes that plague the real swing are there in the practice swing.

Good practice swings are like push-ups. One push-up does nothing, but hundreds of push-ups done on a regular basis have a dramatic effect. Your practice swings are governed by a similar dynamic of repetition. Done correctly, the good practice swing will eventually produce dramatic improvements. Done haphazardly, perhaps instilling Death Moves, bad practice swings will only make improvement that much more elusive.

One breakthrough I have experienced with a broad range of students is to get them to appreciate the value of taking practice swings at home, in the office, or in any setting where they can find just a few minutes, and working on correct body motions. Practice swings from a proper setup to a proper follow-through for brief sessions have brought about significant swing improvements for many. Consistent, short practice sessions are usually much more beneficial than sporadic long sessions. This focused, consistent approach speeds improvement—significantly!

Equally important is the use of drills. Athletes in all sports work on drills to perfect their body actions and tune their muscles. Golf had lagged far behind other sports in this regard. The first book I had published was *Golf Digest's Book of Drills.* I wrote it because there were no books on organized drills. It took years for me to find a publisher, but once it was published, the book became very successful and remains in hardback to this day. I've had hundreds of golf professionals tell me they bring that book to the lesson tee with them nearly every day. Whenever I teach a particular position of the Eight-Step Swing, I find that drills are highly effective. Students quickly learn what to feel and look for when correctly executing each position, and they learn how to arrive at each position. Students also understand that for each position, there is an acceptable variation. That's a vital point.

When changing a position in your swing, it's extremely helpful to view your swing constantly in a mirror or watch it on videotape. It is important that you learn how to look at a golf swing and why good swings don't all look the same. The main reason they look different is that body size, physique, rhythm, tempo, and backswing locations differ so markedly from player to player. Picture the swings of these golfers: Ryan Moore, Curtis Strange, Ben Hogan, Jack Nicklaus, Lorena Ochoa, Nick Price, Sergio Garcia, and Paula Creamer. Obviously, they are not carbon copies of each other, despite the fact that in their own ways, each player achieves the basic fundamental positions I've described in this book. The more you learn what to look for, the true fundamentals, the more the similarities will become apparent.

Can you do it? Can you make a significant swing change or swing adjustment? The answer depends on your determination more than any other factor, but yes, you can. By working with a qualified PGA teaching professional who will help keep you motivated and spot mistakes, most golfers can achieve their own acceptable version of the efficient, powerful golf swing shown in the eight steps. You'll know you are within reach of a consistent, fundamentally correct swing action when you can automatically go through the step or steps you have changed with no mechanical thought.

## THE "FEEL" SIDE: TIMING AND BALANCE

Like all physical gifts, natural balance and fluid rhythm are not parceled out equally to everyone. Yet, they are probably the most important attributes of the athlete. Some players will never achieve that wonderful, graceful ease of motion that has made Sam Snead, Al Geiberger, Bruce Lietzke, Fred Couples, Phil Mickelson, Annika Sorenstam, Ernie Els, Anthony Kim, and Cristie Kerr so much fun to watch. But you can still work toward improving your rhythm and balance. Physical conditioning and flexibility are factors in the achievement of fluid, even-tempo motion.

To improve your balance, rhythm, and tempo further, you should watch and imitate athletes who embody it. Whenever you can watch a top tour player, make sure to do so with an eye toward recording his or her tempo and storing the "tape" in some corner of your mind. When you get back home, let your body sense that same rhythm. This is the best way to smooth out your swing and keep it from being rigid, nonathletic, and mechanical. Sometimes imitation—the old monkey-see, monkey-do—is the best way to learn. When you practice your swing, work hard on the coordination of your body parts. Focus on timing the club, arms, and body evenly. Sense a balance of all your parts, and simplify your motion by using a 1–2–3 count or repeating a tune inside your head.

It's all part of golf's journey of discovery. To enjoy golf to the fullest, you have to learn to enjoy that journey, with all its peaks and valleys and its occasional long plateaus. Reaching the final lofty destination takes a long time and focused attention on practicing the correct movements. It is not the destination, however, that is always most important. Instead, it is the striving and the paths you choose that provide the fun of golf. On some lucky days, you'll feel that you are zipping along in a new Ferrari, headed in the absolutely right direction. Even for the game's greatest players, those moments seem fleeting. But they are as close as anyone ever gets to mastery in golf.

# ABOUT JIM McLEAN

I've had an incredible life in golf since I began playing as a boy in Seattle. My father, John McLean, was a very good player and gave me my first lessons. I went on to have a very good amateur and college career, learned a tremendous amount about the game in my time playing tournaments worldwide as a professional golfer, and found my calling as a teacher of the game.

My mom, Agnes, took me to many tournaments and was a fine golfer herself. Now my wife, Justine, has done the same for our two boys. When they were junior golfers, she taxied them to many events in and out of Florida. It's a big reason Matt and Jon both received four-year scholarships to top universities for golf.

My teaching career really took off when I accepted the Director of Golf position at Doral in 1990 and began my own golf school operation. In 1994, I was named the National PGA of America Teacher of the Year, published the original *The Eight-Step Swing*, and moved permanently to South Florida. Previously, I had split my time between summers at my Sleepy Hollow Country Club job and winters at my golf school with the Doral Golf Resort & Spa.

It would be hard for a club pro to design a better job than I had at Sleepy Hollow. I had a contract for seven months a year at a beautiful twenty-seven-hole facility with a phenomenal membership and a PGA Senior Tour event. We had three hundred golf members, skeet-shooting facilities, eighteen miles of horseback trails, stables that kept fifty horses, a great tennis program, and a large swimming facility. Also, I lived only four minutes from the club, and my family was treated like gold.

At Sleepy Hollow, we had a huge junior golf program for over one hundred children, and our overall teaching program was second to none. At one time, we had three of the top hundred instructors in the world at one private club, plus two other super-qualified teachers. Our membership included the Rockefellers, Bill Murray, Arthur Ashe, top people from Wall Street, and Jim Hand, a past president of the USGA.

It was Mr. Hand who hired me in 1988, along with Max Chapman, who at the time ran Nomura Bank when I held the dual head professional positions at Quaker Ridge Golf Club in Scarsdale, New York (site of the 1997 Walker Cup Matches), and Tamarisk Country Club in Palm Springs, California (site of the Bob Hope Classic).

Mr. Hand spearheaded the development of a new teaching range at Sleepy Hollow, which included my first real Superstation and likely the first video center built directly on a driving range. Previously I had used much smaller rooms to review swings indoors and hit into nets at my first head pro position at Sunningdale Country Club in Scarsdale, New York, and then similar net rooms at Quaker Ridge and Tamarisk. This was a learning center built directly on my teaching side of the Sleepy Hollow range to my specifications, where you could step in and out directly onto the range (and it had three teaching stations). We could hit balls indoors out onto the range and review videotapes sitting down. Creating this learning atmosphere came from knowing Carl Welty and seeing firsthand the benefits of indoor instruction. Learning indoors is a key element to my teaching system, and it is a mainstay at all our golf schools to this day.

Sleepy Hollow was the Grand Central Station of instruction for all the greater New York City area. It was common to have five teachers slamming lessons six days per week. We had all the top players in the metropolitan area coming to Sleepy Hollow, and it wasn't unusual to see Tom Kite, Brad Faxon, Hal Sutton, Mark McCumber, Jerry Pate, Laurie Marten, Peter Jacobsen, Gary Player, or some other tour professional hitting balls at Sleepy Hollow. Kenny Bakst took lessons there and won the U.S. Mid Amateur. George Zahringer was there at least once a week, and he totally dominated tournament golf in the Met Section, winning the Met Amateur six times and the Met Open and the U.S. Mid Am, and qualifying eighteen times for the U.S. Amateur, plus winning every other major amateur event. Club pros like National Club pro champions Darrell Kestner and Mike Burke, as well as Bobby Heins and Bill Davis, among hundreds of others, came to Sleepy Hollow. We taught players who won every major junior, amateur, and senior event in the Met Section.

Besides this, I was playing more golf myself and was enjoying competing.

George Zahringer and I won the National USF&G Skins game in Palm Springs, where I pocketed $61,000. Later, George would play for America on the U.S. Walker Cup Team. My last year in the Met Section, I finished in the top ten in all six events I played, including a runner-up finish in the section championship, the last event I played in the Met Section. In the Metropolitan Pro-Pro Championship, playing with partner Kelly Moser, I shot a 27 for nine holes and a course-record 63 for the day. I had more good rounds those last few years than I had experienced since my college days. Working with one of my instructors, Dave Collins, I used my limited practice time (two jobs, two children, coaching Little League baseball, etc.) very efficiently. In doing so, I definitely learned practice techniques that work great for people without a lot of time, which I have passed on in this book.

I knew that moving to Miami would totally change my life. It would be a full-out commitment to teaching, and I could virtually forget playing competitive golf. Sure, I was already running Doral during the winter months, but this meant no more club professional life. It meant full-time schools, not part-time schools, as I had done since 1985. Yet, I knew this was the way to go, since teaching was the part of golf I loved the most. Without any question, the decision to leave the club pro ranks was the best move of my professional life.

The school at Doral Golf Resort & Spa has grown each and every year. In 1996, our golf school at Doral was rated by *U.S. News & World Report* as the Number One school in America. In 2000, an independent study by CNN also rated us Number One. Best of all, I know we have continued to improve and just recently my school in Ft. Worth was rated the Number One school in Texas (*Golf Magazine*, 2008).

Regarding my golf schools, I now have thirty-four PGA professionals working at my Doral Golf School during the winter months, seventeen PGA professionals at my PGA West Golf School, and five PGA professionals at my La Quinta Golf School. I have golf schools in Phoenix; Traverse City, Michigan; Utah; Toronto; and Madrid. I also own a spectacular golf facility in Fort Worth, Texas. This practice facility is one of the finest all-around instruction sites in the world. All of them are extremely busy with teachers I have personally trained, and we now have had nine instructors rated by *Golf Magazine* among the top one hundred teachers in the world. Thirty-two of my instructors have been ranked as Best in State by *Golf Digest*.

In 1995, I was asked to join the fledging Golf Channel as a Master Instruction Adviser. With a small start-up audience of fewer than two million viewers, I began my career as a TV instructor. Since that time, I have become a regular on the Golf Channel, conducting my own TV show. As I write this, the Golf Channel now has over 100 million viewers. Without a doubt, my many appearances on the Golf Channel exposed my teaching ideas worldwide. It also made me better at detailing ideas, as we shot so many different TV shows.

Doral, where I spend most of my time, is one of the most unbelievable places on earth for golf. Not only do we have five really fine golf courses, but we have a 700-room hotel, 130 vacation villa rooms, and a 48-room world-class spa. The Doral Blue Monster is our most famous course, and it hosts the CA Championship, a World Golf event, each year, open only to the top eighty players in the world. Tiger Woods has won it three times. The Blue is certainly one of the best and most difficult courses the tour plays each year. In the summer of 1999, I was in charge of the bunker restoration (126 new bunkers) on the Blue. We also have Greg Norman's fabulous Great White, which twice hosted the Shark Shoot-Out. The finals of the 1999 PGA Tour Qualifying were held on our Gold and Silver courses. I recently totally redesigned the Silver, adding over five hundred yards of length and recontouring the entire course. It will play as a much tougher test for the top-level players and provide a tournament-capable course. It will become a Jim McLean Signature Course at Doral.

I hope you can visit us at one of our locations. I promise you will experience fantastic teaching. If there is one most important thing I have tried to do, it is to assemble the best staff and the best training of any instruction program in the world. If you come, I am sure you will notice it very quickly.

In this book I have detailed the system I use to teach the golf swing. Remember—a system is not a method. The information contained within serves as a major portion of what my instructors must know to teach at our schools. That, of course, means this is an in-depth study.

I want to mention one more time that we do not teach eight identical steps to our students. Many times I will not even mention the word step. Rather, it is a precision diagnostic tool that breaks down the swing into key checkpoints. When you understand where your swing should be at specific locations, you too can accurately diagnose your own golf swing. With this book you have the tools to dissect the inner workings and components of a powerful and accurate swing action.

To me, steps make the swing understandable. When I first broke the golf swing into body action and club action and combined it with the Corridors of Success, I knew I was on to an entirely new way of helping my students. The bottom line is my system works. We prove it every day at all our schools, and we have been doing it for a long time.

When you get right down to it, great teaching is simply the ability to consistently help people improve. *A top teacher can do it time after time with any type of student.* That's what I call "total game instruction," and improving the full golf swing is probably the most fun aspect of it all. With the Eight-Step System I've seen a wide range of instructors have tremendous success with all types of students. I'm also very confident this system will work for you.

The golf swing is complex, but we need to make it understandable and as simple as we possibly can. The only way I know to do this is by learning, understanding, and then executing the true fundamentals and the basic moves that golf demands.

Remember to break the golf swing down to an action you can master. Then build on that success. The building block approach is something that great coaches use in all sports.

Enjoy the journey.

—*Jim McLean*

## JIM McLEAN'S PLAYING RESUME

- Qualified for all the major USGA events: the U.S. Junior, the U.S. Amateur (4), the U.S. Open (2), and the U.S. Senior Open
- Made the cut at the Masters
- Won the Northwest Open
- Won the Pacific Northwest Amateur three times
- Won the Pacific Coast Am at Olympic Club in San Francisco
- Won the Westchester PGA
- Runner-up in the Metropolitan PGA
- Won the National Skins Game at PGA West with amateur partner George Zahringer ($61,000 first prize)

- Qualified for ten National Club Pro Championships
- Won the Metropolitan Pro-Pro Championship two times
- Shot 27 for nine holes in a tournament and 63 for a course record
- Held three course records at Doral during one period
- Has won over fifty junior and amateur events, including the Washington State Junior two times
- Played 203 holes in one day for charity, with a low round of 66
- Received a four-year full scholarship to the University of Houston under legendary coach Dave Williams (16 NCAA championships)
- Had the low scoring average at Houston his senior year
- Received All-American status
- Played on teams that included John Mahaffey (PGA champion), Bruce Lietzke (U.S. Senior Open champion), Bill Rogers (British Open champion ranked Number One in the world in 1981), Fuzzy Zoeller (U.S. Open champion and Masters champion), Tom Jenkins, Keith Fergus, Lanny Wadkins, Bruce Ashworth, and Bobby Walzel
- Inducted into the Pacific Northwest Hall of Fame in 2003

## OVERVIEW OF JIM McLEAN'S TEACHING RESUME

- Jim taught four U.S. Open Women's champions.
- Jim taught Men's U.S. Open champion Tom Kite.
- Jim has taught seven Juniors who have reached the Number One ranking in America.
- Jim has taught over a hundred PGA Tour professionals.
- Jim has taught hundreds of top Junior players.
- Jim has taught hundreds of top amateur players.
- Jim's schools are the undisputed Number One–rated golf school in America.

# ACKNOWLEDGMENTS

This book had to be updated, it had to be upgraded, and it had to be written. I spent years writing notes and new material based on *The Eight-Step Swing*. Once it was completed, the amount of words was overwhelming, so I asked a great old friend to help slice it down into something a publisher would accept. That person is Jaime Diaz, one of golf's top writers, who formerly wrote for the *New York Times* and now writes for *Golf Digest*. I've always admired his wonderful writing style and his golf insight. I also love the fact that he grew up next door to one of my favorite golf courses, the San Francisco Golf Club, where he would, as a junior golfer, often sneak on for a few holes of golf. Jaime is a very good golfer himself and has delved deeply into the game. I knew he was the perfect person to help write my most important book.

My friend and world class artist, Phil Franke, has provided the new drawings that explode off the pages. A huge thanks to Phil. Also my current assistant, Eric Lillibridge, and the rest of the professionals on my teaching staffs. All of them have contributed to this book.

Although this book does include all of my latest work on the eight steps, there is so much more. I've tried to give you the very best (the building blocks) of what we teach at our golf schools and show you why our schools are so successful with every level of golfer.

—*Jim McLean*